Social Reform Movements to Protect

America's Vulnerable 1830–1940

WOMEN &
CHILDREN
First

*Edited by David J. Rothman and
Sheila M. Rothman*

A Garland Series

THE CONSUMERS' LEAGUE OF NEW YORK
BEHIND THE SCENES OF WOMEN'S WORK

Edited by David J. Rothman and Sheila M. Rothman

Garland Publishing, Inc.
New York & London
1987

For a complete list of the titles in this series
see the final pages of this volume.

The facsimile of *Behind the Scenes in a Restaurant* is from a copy in the New
York Public Library; that of *Behind the Scenes in a Hotel* is from a copy in the
Yale University Library; that of *Behind the Scenes in Canneries* is from a copy in
the Buffalo Public Library.

Library of Congress Cataloging-in-Publication Data

The Consumers' League of New York.

(Women & children first)
Reprint (1st work). Originally published: Behind the scenes in a restaurant.
[New York] : Consumers' League of New York, 1916.
Reprint (2nd work). Originally published: Behind the scenes in a hotel. New
York City : Consumers' League of New York, 1922.
Reprint (3rd work). Originally published: Behind the scenes in canneries.
New York City : Consumers' League of New York, 1930.
1. Women—Employment—New York (State) I. Rothman, David J.
II. Rothman, Sheila M. III. Consumers' League of New York City. IV. Be-
hind the scenes in a restaurant. 1987. V. Behind the scenes in a hotel.
1987. VI. Behind the scenes in canneries. 1987. VII. Series.
HD6096.N6C66 1987   331.4'2'09747   87-19804
ISBN 0-8240-7684-2 (alk. paper)

The volumes in this series are printed on
acid-free, 250-year-life paper.

Printed in the United States of America.

Behind the Scenes in a Restaurant
The Consumers' League of New York City

Behind the Scenes in a Hotel
The Consumers' League of New York City

Behind the Scenes in Canneries
The Consumers' League of New York City

EDITORS' NOTE

These pamphlets provide a comprehensive portrait of the conditions under which women worked in New York City. Focusing on women employees in restaurants, hotels, and canneries, this material provides important statistical information on the background of these women and their hours of labor and work conditions. It demonstrates why protective legislation became a primary item on the reform agenda.

D.J.R.
S.M.R.

Behind the Scenes in a Restaurant

A Study of 1017 Women Restaurant Employees

By

The Consumers' League of New York City

1916

TABLE OF CONTENTS.

Wanted—A Rest

FOREWORD.

"I keep hearing about laws for women. Where are they?" This was the question asked by a woman working twelve hours a day in a restaurant. What must we tell her? What excuse have we to offer for excluding her from the protection the law gives to women working in factories and mercantile establishments? That we have safeguarded women in these fields of employment from overwork proves that we know the dangers of overwork, that long hours interpreted in terms of human life mean exhaustion, disease, immorality, pauperism and a weaker generation to follow our own. This is an old story, it has been told again and again. Yet with our over-sensitiveness to an encroachment upon the rights and liberties of American citizens, we have failed to extend the protection of our laws to all who need their protection.

The New York State Labor Law as it stands makes it illegal to employ women in factories and mercantile establishments more than fifty-four hours or six days in any one week, or between ten o'clock at night and six o'clock in the morning. So far, so good. If these laws are enforced, we may feel fairly confident that women in these branches of industry at least have some measure of protection. But what of the women not safeguarded by the law? Who are they, and why should they be neglected?

Between fifteen and twenty thousand of these women are workers in restaurants—waitresses, cooks, kitchen girls, pantry hands—upon whose services all of us depend at one time or another for our comfort and pleasure. The Consumers' League of New York City has long felt the need of including restaurant workers under the provisions of the Labor Law. The State Department of Labor lays special stress upon this need.* Believing, therefore, both from casual observation and from the statement of the Labor Department that women in restaurants are not properly guarded from industrial strain, the League planned to explore the field further, to discover just what actually are the hours, wages and general conditions

---

* See Appendix I.

of work in this branch of industry and to learn their effect upon the life and health of the worker.

A valuable study of this subject was made in 1910 by the United States Bureau of Labor Statistics for New York and several of the larger cities of the country.* Though the Consumers' League has not entered upon wholly new ground, yet with adequate time for detailed study it has been possible for it to make a more exhaustive inquiry than any made heretofore, and to bring to light new phases of the question. The story of its discoveries is told in the pages that follow, to this end, that with wider knowledge of facts, public interest may be reawakened and stimulated to demand adequate legal protection for women employed in restaurants.

---

*Women and Child Wage-earners in the United States, Vol. V., Chap. X.

PLAN OF STUDY.

Believing that one of the most satisfactory sources of information in regard to labor conditions is the word of the workers themselves, the Consumers' League decided to base its study mainly upon interviews with restaurant employees. One thousand and seventeen (1,017) women were interviewed in New York City and in six of the larger cities of the State. They were seen in their homes, at their places of employment and through employment agencies.

In New York City all the interviews were held at the Occupational Clinic of the Board of Health, where, through the courtesy of Dr. Harris, Chief of the Bureau of Industrial Hygiene, a room was set aside for the use of the League investigator. In response to a requirement of the Health Department, all food-handlers in the city come to the Clinic for a physical examination and certificate testifying that they are free from communicable disease. The investigator could in this way meet the women on neutral ground when there was no temptation to conceal or distort facts, and talk confidentially with them. The interviews taken at the Clinic in five months would have required at least a year to get in any other way.

The New York State Consumers' League and the branch leagues in Buffalo, Syracuse and Mr. Vernon co-operated in interviewing women in localities outside of New York City, and the same undesirable conditions were found to prevail throughout the State.

Supplementary information was also obtained from all other available sources, such as employers, employment agencies, girls' clubs and published reports. The workers came from every kind of restaurant, including hotels, tea-rooms, buffet and dairy lunches, cafeterias and clubs. In this way it was possible to get in touch with a thoroughly representative group of workers, including the best paid as well as the most underpaid.

In undertaking the investigation, the League sought to answer three questions: first, what are the actual conditions of labor prevailing in the restaurants of New York State; second, are these conditions such that the worker may lead a wholesome, normal life; and third, how do these conditions react through the individual worker upon society as a whole.

The Consumers' League acknowledges its deep indebtedness to Dr. Harris for the helpful interest that he has taken in its work, and for his courtesy in allowing the League investigator to take interviews at the Occupational Clinic.

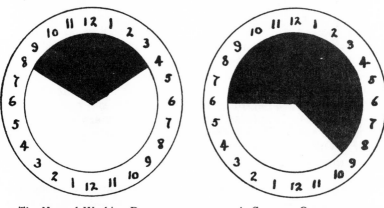

The Normal Working Day—
Eight Hours.

A Common Occurrence—
Fifteen Hours.

There is no class of employees who serve the public so directly as do restaurant workers. Also, it is obviously of vital interest to the public that those who serve them in this way be strong and healthy since they are in a position peculiarly adapted to spread disease. The study just terminated has brought to light certain facts which point to a grave danger to the individual worker, to those whom she serves and to the community. Hard work kept up for incredibly long hours, low pay, health impaired and resistance to disease lowered through fatigue—these are some of the facts which make action on our part necessary, that restaurant work may be a safe and wholesome occupation.

THE WORKER.

AGE.

An outstanding feature of restaurant work is the presence in this occupation of a very large proportion of girls and young women. One-fourth of all the workers are under 21, and two-thirds under 30 years of age. (See Diagram 1). There are several reasons to account for this fact.

A certain amount of excitement attaches to the work of a restaurant waitress which appeals to young girls. She sees and talks to a great many people; she likes the noise and bustle and cheerful atmosphere of the dining room. Also, the employer prefers young and pretty girls as waitresses, especially where the customers are mostly men. They help to make his place attractive and popular. One waitress remarked, "When the girls get to looking bad, they are laid off and someone else is put in their place."

As might be expected, restaurant cooks are a somewhat older set of women than the waitresses, not quite one-half being under 30 years. Their work requires experience and the ability to think and plan. Considering the nature and demands of the work, it is startling to find that twenty per cent. of their number are girls not yet 21 years old.

Over seventy-five per cent. of the kitchen girls and other helpers* are under 30, and nearly half under 21. This is the youngest group. Their work needs no skill or previous training, the chief requirement being physical strength.

The youth of these restaurant workers gives rise to two distinct dangers, a physical danger and a moral one. Restaurant work necessarily involves many hours of standing and walking, lifting and carrying heavy weights. This is an unavoidable feature, but it is of the utmost importance that it be not ignored. Medical authorities have pointed out the serious results that follow the strain of continued standing and over-work of young girls. Dr. Harris states that in occupations which require such

---

* Dishwashers, silver cleaners, tray girls, cashiers, laundry workers and pantry hands are included in this term.

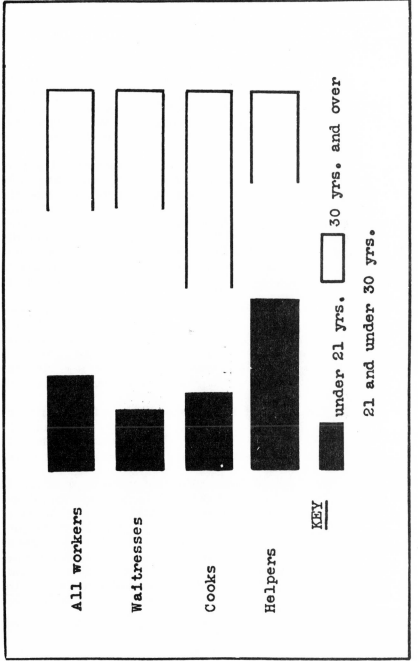

DIAGRAM 1.—Ages of Women Employed in Restaurants by Occupation.

lifting and carrying and such long hours of standing "there is a definite hazard to the child-bearing capacity of women. This is of vital consequence to society as a whole."

The moral danger of the work is largely confined to waitresses. Because of their position, they are peculiarly exposed to the attentions of men customers. For this very reason, the Baltimore Vice Commission recommends that only older and more experienced women be employed in this capacity, while in Norway the law sets a minimum age limit for waitresses in public places.

If the restaurant worker is to resist the strain of the work and the temptations to which she is exposed, hours and conditions must be so adjusted as to prevent all overtaxing of her strength and elasticity.

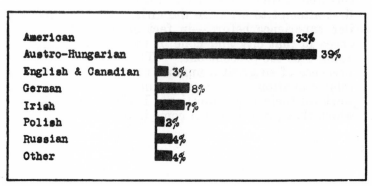

DIAGRAM 2.—Nationality of Women Restaurant Workers.

NATIONALITY.

The majority of restaurant workers are foreigners. Less than one-third are American-born, and of these a great many have foreign-born parents and live among members of their own race, so that they can hardly be classed as Americans. The largest single group is made up of Austro-Hungarians. (See Diagram 2). The demand for cheap, unskilled labor in this occupation calls for the kind of service which these girls and others of the European peasant class can give. The outdoor life in the fields of their native land fits them for the hard labor required in a restaurant kitchen. They do not remain fit long, however. After a year or two of this work, much of their sturdiness is lost, color and brightness are gone from their faces, and they have become pale and listless. A curiously dull, passive look is characteristic of many of them.

Living as they do among their own people these young peasants have no opportunity to absorb American standards and customs. Their ignorance makes it easy for employers to exploit them, demanding hours of labor and paying wages to which no American girl would submit. An employment agent said: "My 'phone rings day and night—all want peasant girls for kitchen helpers because they are the only kind that will stand such long hours." Attempts to organize restaurant workers in New York State have never succeeded. The Secretary of the Hotel and Restaurant Employees' International Alliance, speaking of their unsuccessful efforts along

8

this line in New York City in 1915, says, "This is not the first attempt to organize the girls. We have had a similar experience before,—in fact have had three experiences in that city and none of them a bit more encouraging that the present one." This is largely due to the presence of so great a number of young foreign girls in this occupation. They are not in a position to unite and work for their own protection. The only channel through which that protection can come is the law.

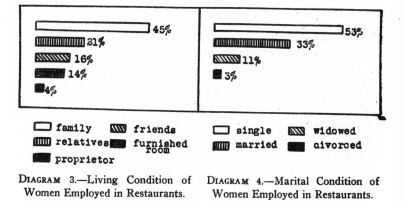

DIAGRAM 3.—Living Condition of Women Employed in Restaurants.

☐ family	▨ friends
▥ relatives	▦ furnished room
▰ proprietor	

DIAGRAM 4.—Marital Condition of Women Employed in Restaurants.

☐ single	▨ widowed
▥ married	▰ divorced

FAMILY AND HOME.

While the greater number of restaurant workers are unmarried, it is rather surprising to find so large a proportion of married women in the work. (See Diagram 4.) This is easily explained, however, by the fact that many of them are "one-meal" girls, that is, they are employed only for the rush hour at noon. In this way they can earn a little extra money while their husbands are at work, either as "pin-money" for themselves, or to help toward the support of the children.

The majority of restaurant employees live with their family or relatives (See Diagram 3), but this does not mean that they are not entirely self-dependent. As large a proportion of a girl's wage goes into the family exchequer as she would have to pay for board and lodging elsewhere. The financial advantage of living at home appears chiefly in giving her a place of refuge when she is out of a job.

Restaurant workers are a tenement house population. A few, to be sure, can afford comfortable little apartments of their own, but as a whole their lot falls within the congested tenement districts of the city. Confusion, over-crowding, dirt, lack of sunlight, air and privacy, and unwholesome surroundings are only too common in their homes. The janitor of an East Side tenement house said: "A little while ago down in Third Street there were twenty-three girls sleeping in two rooms. They'd put their matresses down on the floor at night and pile them on top of each other in the day time. Most of them were kitchen hands at_____'s," naming a well-known chain of restaurants.

The low standards of the European peasant class from which restaurant workers are largely recruited, drag down all standards. No other result is possible under present conditions. They live—but how? Low wages, miserably long hours, no opportunity to fit themselves for their new surroundings—this is what we offer these young peasant girls who come to America confidently expecting better things than they have left behind.

HOURS.

WEEKLY HOURS OF LABOR.

The salient characteristic of restaurant work is the length of the working day. Fifty-eight per cent. of the women employees work each week beyond the fifty-four-hour limit set by law for women in stores and factories. A twelve-hour day and a seven-day week is the lot of one-fifth of these workers. (See Diagram 5.) A fifteen-hour day is not uncommon. Not quite one-half of the wait-resses work over 54 hours a week or 9 hours a day. The reason for this is that a large number of them, 31 per cent., are "one-meal girls." *Seventy-eight per cent.* of all other restaurant workers, however, exceed the fifty-four hour week.

Comparing the hours of labor of these women with the hours of labor of all employees, both male and female, in the factories of New York State, four per cent. of the factory employees and thirty-five per cent. of the women restaurant employees work over sixty hours a week. Two per cent. of the factory employees and twenty per cent. of the women in restaurants work seventy-two hours or over.*

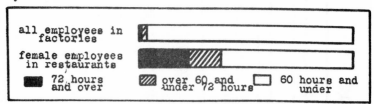

DIAGRAM 6.—Comparison of Weekly Hours of Labor for Women in Restaurants and all Factory Employees in New York State.

Shorter hours have been brought about in factories by the voluntary action of manufacturers, who recognize the inefficiency of over-worked men and women; by concerted action of the workers, who have united to fight for their own protection; and by legal enactment, proving that the people of New York State are alive to the dangers of overwork. Some restaurant managers realize the waste and harm of too long hours and arrange their

---

* 13th U. S. Census, 1910, Vol. VIII, Manufactures, p. 314

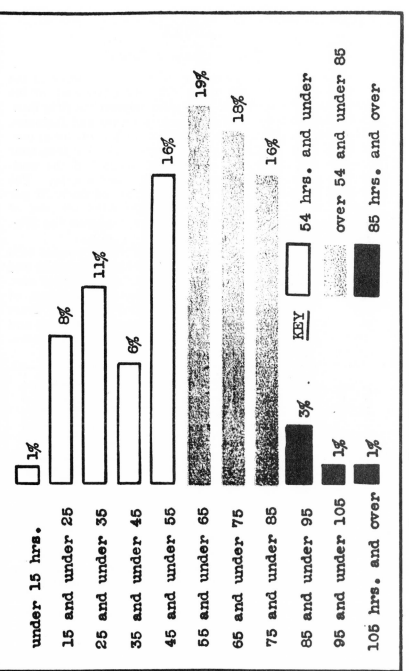

DIAGRAM 5.—Weekly Hours of Labor of Women Employed in Restaurants.

employees' time accordingly; most of them do not. Women restaurant workers in New York State have never been successfully organized; they cannot protect themselves. They have no legal redress for overwork; the law has neglected them. In the course of this investigation, a girl of twenty was found working one hundred and twenty-two hours a week—longer than the law allows factory employees to work in two weeks. Yet this is within the law. Although restaurants differ from stores and factories in keeping open more hours a day, and sometimes for the whole twenty-four, a system of shifts would do away with the scandalously long hours to which thousands of girls and women are bound.

That restaurant work is at best a great drain upon the phyisical strength and nervous force of the worker is evident. Standing, walking, lifting and carrying heavy weights is unavoidable. The report on restaurants made by the United States Bureau of Labor Statistics says: "There was much complaint among the waitresses that the work was very hard and they could stand it but a few years. A number of the girls interviewed had worked as three meal girls until their health was broken; then they took positions as one meal girls and barely made a living. Carrying the heavy trays and the constant standing and walking cause ill health. Usually a man is employed to carry away the empty dishes, but the waitresses must bring the trays loaded with food."*

Besides the cost to endurance, nerves are at constant tension for hurry is the remorseless rule. A waitress must not only remember a multitude of orders and fill them quickly, but she must keep her temper under the exactions of the most trying customer. The cook must keep her head amid the confusion and noise of a hot, crowded kitchen. The kitchen girl must be everywhere at once with a helping hand and the dish-washer's very job depends upon her quickness. One of this latter group said that she washes seven thousand articles in an hour and a half. A waitress, when asked the effect of the work upon her, answered, "Sore feet and a devilish mean disposition." A man restaurant worker speaking of kitchen girls remarked, "It's no work for a woman. They have to lift heavy pots full of vegetables and fill

---

*Women and Child Wage-earners in the United States. Vol. V, p. 199.

in all the gaps. A man has some endurance, but a woman can't stand it more than nine hours a day.''

Many kinds of work are difficult and taxing in their performance, but if the working day is not prolonged beyond a certain point, and there is a sufficient period of rest, such work is not necessarily injurious to the health of the worker. If this point is passed, health is impaired.

A MOVIE
OF THE RESTAURANT WORKER

I
7 A.M.
The Waitress arrives –15 minutes for breakfast

II
7.15 to 10 A.M.
Customers must be served

III
10 to 12 A.M.
She sorts folds and polishes

IV
12 to 3 P.M.
With heavy trays she walks about five miles

V
3 to 5 P.M.
"Free" and nowhere to go

VI
5 to 8 P.M.
Carrying trays and walking many miles

VII
9 P.M.
Exhausted Home and to bed

VIII
6 A.M.
The daily grind begins again

HER PROGRAM FOR ⟨ ELEVEN HOURS A DAY! SEVEN DAYS A WEEK!

The day of a restaurant worker does not begin with her arrival at the restaurant nor end when she leaves. Half of these women live at a distance, taking thirty minutes or more to reach their place of employment. When this extra hour spent in going to and from work is added to a twelve hour day, it is a factor to be reckoned with. It means cutting off an already insufficient night's rest, and, when a girl cannot afford carfare, a weary walk home after being on her feet all day. Nor is this all. Only a few of the best-paid waitresses can afford to pay for the laundering of their aprons and uniforms. Consequently this must be done by the girl herself, adding another burden to a load already too heavy.

The law requires that girls in factories and stores have at least one-half hour off for luncheon. This does not apply to restaurant workers. The "one-meal" girls eat before and after serving, but the majority of the "two-meal" and full-time girls have no time at all for meals. They must eat when they can snatch a moment from their work. There were many complaints of indigestion and loss of appetite from the workers as a result of haste and irregularity in taking their meals. One girl remarked, "You're glad to grab 'em any way you can round here," and another said, "It's a wonder more girls aren't dead, the way they eat all of a rush. Often the smell of food all the time takes away my appetite so I can't eat any way."

A regular time off for meals would be of great benefit to the worker not only in allowing her to eat quietly and comfortably, but in giving her a little rest. In some restaurants after the noon rush is over the girls can sit down and do "side-work," folding napkins, polishing silver, filling salt-cellars, etc. The greater number of girls, however, have no so-called "idle time." They must be on their job continuously. In other restaurants the girls work on a "split trick," that is, they have one or two hours off in the afternoon. This is a very unpopular arrangement. Not only does it keep them out late in the evening, but they cannot use their free time to good advantage. There is little opportunity for recreation or social intercourse during these hours because they come in the morning or afternoon when the girls' friends are all at work. Nor is there ordinarily time for fresh air and exercise, especially in the case of the kitchen workers. A waitress usually has only to take off her apron to be ready for the street, but the other women have not time to change to street clothes and back again in their free period. They stay in the hot kitchen because no other place is provided.

Up at six, away at 6:30, home at 8 o'clock at night worn out by the wear and tear of twelve hours' toil, a dress and an apron to be washed and ironed for to-morrow—after a day like this, what spirit or strength is left to a girl for play and the friendly relations that safeguard her from moral danger? It is a significant fact that with few exceptions the restaurant worker is not known to settlements and girls' clubs. She does not share the group interests and social life open to other working girls. Neither does she make friends with her fellow-workers—the spring and vitality needed to win and establish friendships has been lost under the deadening effect of overwork.

According to Miss Mary Van Kleeck's estimate in her study of "Working Girls in Evening Schools," less than one per cent. of those attending were restaurant workers. They simply have not the physical strength for outside activities and interests. Time after time in answer to the question "What do you do in the evening?" came the reply, "Oh, I go right to bed." One girl, who left the work because of broken health, said, "If I went out in the evening I'd be sick the next day, and the boss would say I couldn't expect to do good work if I stayed out late at night."

The report on restaurants of the Chicago Juvenile Protective Association, emphasizes a truth too much ignored when it says: "The entire investigation revealed once more the hideous risks of the excessively fatigued and overworked girl, who is able to obtain the rest and comfort she craves only through illicit channels."[*]

---

[*] The Girl Employed in Hotels and Restaurants. Juvenile Protective Association of Chicago, 1912.

16

Restaurant Kitchen Opening on Row of Toilets.

Although the number of women employed in restaurants at night is not great, night work in this occupation is a factor to be seriously considered. The restaurants which employ women at night are the small establishments in the tenement districts of the city where hours are longest and surroundings most trying; the cheaper restaurants in the theatre districts where the employment of women is an added attraction to after-the-theatre supper parties; and restaurants in railway stations which are necessarily open all night.

The law makes it illegal to employ women in factories and mercantile establishments between 10 p. m. and 6 a. m. The reasons which caused the state to exercise its police power to safeguard the health and morals of these classes of workers apply equally to the employment of women in restaurants. The very fact that only four per cent. of the workers interviewed were employed at night proves that night work for women in restaurants is not a necessary evil. That it is an evil is beyond question.

The dangers of night work are two-fold. First, it is a distinct menace to the health of the worker. The Factory Investigating Commission in its Report to the Legislature for 1913, states: "The chief danger to health from night work is . . . due to the inevitable lack of sleep and sunlight. Recuperation from fatigue takes place fully only in sleep, and best in sleep at night. Hence night work is, in a word, against nature. This injury to health is all the greater because sleep lost at night by working women is never fully made up by day. For, in the first place, sleep in the day time is not equal in recuperative power to sleep at night. . . . Moreover, quiet and privacy for sleep by day is almost impossible to secure. Upon returning home in the middle of the night or at dawn the workers can snatch at most only a few hours' rest."

Often a woman will have one week of night work alternating with a week of work in the day time. She hardly gets accustomed to sleeping by day when she is taken off the night shift, to change back again at the end of the week. Thus it is impossible for her to form regular habits in sleeping and eating.

Secondly, there is a grave moral danger involved in

17

night work, especially for restaurant workers since at this time they are open to the attentions of an undesirable class of men. "I don't like to work at night," one young waitress said. "The men are always fresher to girls at night than in the day time. Perhaps it's because so many of those gamblers come in drunk." Nor is it safe for a woman to go home alone after twelve o'clock at night. Instances of hideous occurrences are familiar to everyone. A little widow, the mother of seven children, told the investigator that she had given up her work as a dishwasher for this very reason. A friend of hers working in a nearby restaurant, was set upon, robbed and killed on her way home from work late one night. "I changed my work then," said the woman, "for what would the children do if anything happened to me?"

The majority of restaurants employ men for night duty. It is evident, therefore, that the employment of women is not essential to the convenience and comfort of either restaurant owners or customers.

In nearly every branch of industry the working week is six days long. It is universally conceded that there must be one day in the seven for rest and relaxation if men and women are to give their best service. With restaurant workers, thirty-three per cent. of whom have no day of rest in seven, the need for such a time is particularly great because of the long working day. Otherwise they have no opportunity for a thorough rest and the poisons of fatigue are not thrown off. If these poisons are not eliminated, they accumulate in the system and finally result in physical breakdown.

And not only is this free day important on the score of health, but it is also the time for recreation and the strengthening of family ties. For the girl who has no leisure, no time for real relaxation and play, there is only a starved and empty existence. A woman who has no opportunity to be with and to know her children, who must leave them to the care of friends or a day nursery or the street, who has no day in the week to be at home with them, can hardly be a potent factor in shaping their lives. She suffers and so do the children, and the stability of such a family life is at best uncertain. One woman said, "If I get a half day off on Sunday to be with my children, it makes me happy all the week."

18

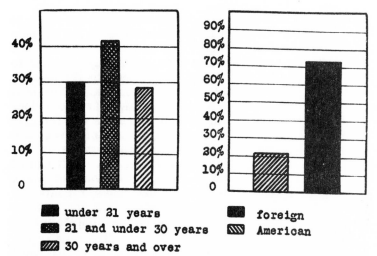

DIAGRAM 7.—Ages of Women Restaurant Workers Employed Over 54 Hours Weekly.

DIAGRAM 8.—Nationality of Women Restaurant Workers Employed Over 54 Hours Weekly.

THE LONG-DAY WORKERS.

Who are the workers that bear the brunt of the long hours in restaurants? They are for the most part the younger women and girls—those who are most likely to be injured by overstrain. They are the very ones whom it is to society's interest to protect most carefully since by their strength is measured the strength of the next generation. Less than thirty per cent. of all workers exceeding fifty-four hours a week are over thirty years of age. (See Diagram 7.)

Foreign-born women also make up the greater part of this group. (See Diagram 8.) They do not know how to protect themselves from employers' unreasonable demands, they must have work and they are not trained for anything except unskilled labor. They will work any number of hours exacted by the employer whatever the cost, until exhaustion renders them unfit for labor of any kind.

WAGES.

WEEKLY WAGES.

The wage of restaurant workers is of immediate interest to everyone who enters a restaurant. You not only pay for your food, but your tip helps to pay the waitress's salary. It is upon this source of income that she depends for the greater part of her earnings. Any study of wages in this branch of industry must take into consideration not only that tips form a large part of the income of waitresses but that the majority of women get all their meals at the restaurant, or the equivalent of $3.00 a week in addition to actual wages.* Professor Streightoff has fixed upon $9.00 a week as the minimum amount upon which a girl can live independently in New York City.† Eighty-seven per cent of all women restaurant workers are being paid less than $9.00, but when food and tips are estimated and added, the proportion receiving less than a living wage is thirty-one per cent. While it is true therefore that the majority of workers in restaurants are earning enough to support themselves, it is a matter for grave concern that so large a number of women are being forced below the lowest point at which they can maintain health and decency.

Moreover this $9.00 a week minimum does not allow for saving against illness, dentist's bills, unemployment or any other emergency. Taking $10.00 a week as the least upon which a girl can live and save, we find that forty-nine per cent. of these women are receiving in actual wages or their equivalent less than this amount. A few restaurant workers live at their place of employment, thus receiving lodging as well as board, but as this is true of only four per cent., the proportion is too small to affect appreciably the wage scale as a whole.

It is upon the kitchen and pantry hands who make up twenty-eight per cent. of all the workers that the burden of low wages falls most heavily. Waitresses have the opportunity to make tips, cooks receive comparatively fair wages because their work requires a certain amount

---

* Report of the State Factory Investigating Commission for 1915, Vol. IV, p. 1593.
  † *Ibid.*, p. 1609.

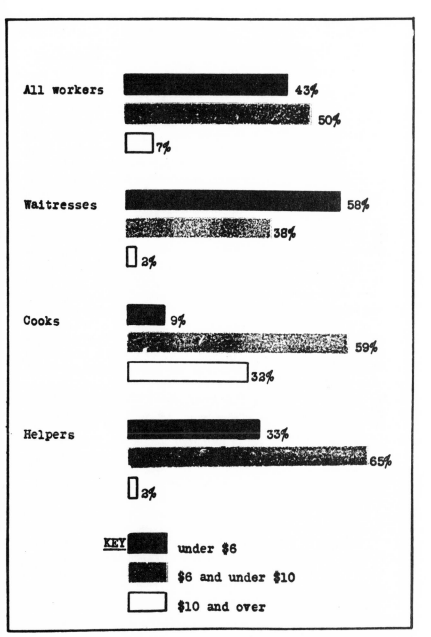

DIAGRAM 9.—Weekly Wages of Women Employed in Restaurants.

of skill, but the other women cannot make tips and their unskilled labor is very poorly paid. One-third are receiving less than $6.00 a week, and three-fourths less than $7.00. (See Diagram 9.)

The income of a restaurant worker is not clear gain. Certain expenses are involved in the work which she must meet herself. In restaurants where a special dress is required the waitress must provide her own uniforms, and she must also either wash them herself, or pay for having them laundered. Two clean uniforms a week is the usual requirement and in some cases three. The report of the United States Labor Department estimates that it costs a girl about $0.63 a week for the laundering of her aprons alone.* It costs $0.25 to have a uniform laundered, which means $1.13 must be deducted from the $3.50 a week usually paid to waitresses in tea-rooms, where special dresses are always required. In one New York tea-room the girls must have two sets of uniforms, a white dress with white shoes, and a blue dress with black shoes. Each uniform costs $2.50.

Fines also eat into the restaurant worker's earnings. Girls are commonly fined for lateness, one particular restaurant exacting $0.25 if a girl is ten minutes late. Her pay is always cut for breakage, and in some places a certain amount is deducted weekly whether she breaks any dishes or not. Also, mistakes in adding up checks, either over or under the correct amount, and mistakes in orders, must be paid for by the waitress. "Those are the things that make the girls mad," said one. In one New York tea-room this summer, a customer was served with hot coffee, when she had asked for iced tea, the waitress misunderstanding the order. The mistake was corrected and the iced tea substituted. When the waitress brought the customer her check, however, both tea and coffee were charged, and the girl laid down twenty cents upon the table. "You know, we have to pay for our mistakes," she said.

What low wages mean in actual living cannot be expressed by figures. Poor quarters in questionable parts of the city, clothing of the most utilitarian kind, no money for the pretty things that every well-constituted girl wants, nothing for recreation, and worst of all, debts

---

* Women and Child Wage-earners, Vol. V, p. 362.

after illness or unemployment which take the very heart out of a girl in the bitter struggle to pay them off. The proprietor of a Buffalo employment agency remarked, "Look at the Wants Ads; with the many factories in Buffalo you will find the list "Help Wanted for Restaurants" equals that of "Help Wanted for Factory Work," and what does that mean?—Simply that the restaurant workers are a discontented lot and all because of the excessively long hours and low wages."

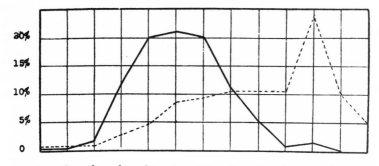

DIAGRAM 10.—Comparison of Weekly Wages (black line) and Weekly Income (dotted line) of Waitresses in Restaurants.

THE TIPPING SYSTEM.

Tipping is a direct drag upon wages. When the public is perfectly willing to contribute part of a waitress's wage, why should not the employer take advantage of this fact and pay her less? That is surely to be expected and is almost universally the case. Many girls, accustomed to making a good deal in tips or "scale," as they call it, would not be willing to work for $9.00 a week and no tips, for they can often make more than this amount. But the better class of girl would prefer a living wage and no tips. As matters stand now, however, they are a very necessary part of a girl's income.

Comparing the weekly wage and the weekly income of waitresses as shown in Diagram 10, we find that without tips only 8 per cent. make as much as $9.00 a week, while with tips 50 per cent. receive $9.00 or more. The custom of tipping has two distinct disadvantages. First, it is an unreliable source of income. A girl may reasonably expect to make a certain amount in tips, but she cannot count upon doing so. The danger here is not only that she will receive less than it is possible for her to live on, but that she will get into debt, trusting to luck that her tips will be large enough to get her out. It is very easy to be over-confident. A tea-room waitress said: "Sometimes I make $12.00 a week in tips, sometimes almost nothing. You can't depend on people." Tea-rooms are the greatest sinners in respect to making their waitresses depend upon tips. The usual wage in several of the well-known New York tea-rooms is $3.50 a week for full time, which is ten or twelve hours a day.

23

The other aspect of tipping presents a more subtle danger. The girls need the money and they deliberately work for it, partly by good service, and partly by adopting an intimate personal tone toward their men customers. This leads naturally to familiarity on the man's part and establishes a personal relation between them. Most of the girls quite frankly admit making "dates" with strange men. In one restaurant a woman was pointed out in incredulous admiration by the other waitresses. "Her husband has been dead four years, and she hasn't gone out with a man yet," they said. These "dates" are made with no thought on the part of the girl beyond getting the good time which she cannot afford herself, but the outcome is often a tragedy. The restaurants in one city of the state forbid unnecessary conversation between waitress and customer because conditions resulting from the practice became so flagrant. The result of this custom is that girls are approached to whom any attention from their men customers is most distasteful. The report of the United States Bureau of Labor Statistics says: "Many of the waitresses complain of the annoying attention of male customers. Many girls said, however, that if they speak sharply to a customer or offend him, they are likely to be reprimanded by the head waitress and may even lose their position."*

The Juvenile Protective Association of Chicago considers tipping a vicious system. "The giving of tips should be abolished because of their pernicious effect. A young girl who under any other circumstances would not dream of accepting money from a man will accept it in the guise of a tip. In the hands of a vicious man this tip establishes between him and the girl a relation of subserviency and patronage which may easily be made the beginning of improper attentions. The most conscientious girl, dependent upon tips to eke out her slender wage, finds it difficult to determine just where the line of propriety is crossed. Thus, in addition to the other dangers surrounding the girls employed in hotels and restaurants, they encounter the lack of respect which curiously attaches itself to one who accepts a gratuity."†

* Women and Child Wage-earners in the United States, Vol. V, p. 199.
† The Girl Employed in Hotels and Restaurants. Juvenile Protective Association of Chicago, 1912.

no time unemployed	45%
less than 3 weeks	14%
3 weeks and less than 1 month	13%
1 month and less than 3 months	15%
3 months and over	13%

DIAGRAM 11.—Length of Time Unemployed in Past Year.*

IRREGULARITY OF EMPLOYMENT.

Closely connected with the question of wages is the possibility of being out of a job. If a girl is earning $10.00 a week she may be able, with the most careful saving, to lay aside enough to tide her over two or three weeks of unemployment. But the savings from a $10.00 weekly wage do not last long. Twenty-eight per cent. of these women were out of work one month or longer in the past year because of the slack season, illness, change of their place of employment or for some other reason. The girl who cannot save is in a desperate condition indeed. For her, prolonged unemployment means debt, heart breaking anxiety and dependence.

Girls in restaurant work do not get vacations with pay except in very rare instances. One well-known New York firm having tea-rooms in various parts of the city, is to be congratulated on the fact that it does give its waitresses a vacation with pay. A few of the married women, or those who have families to care for them, can afford to take time out of the year's work for a rest. But when a girl is not working, it is for the most part a matter of stern necessity and inevitably means a time of struggle and suffering.

Restaurants do not labor under the difficulties of seasonal employment. We should expect to find a steadiness in this occupation which the facts do not bear out. It is therefore evident that the instability of the work and constant shifting is due to the unsatisfactory nature of the employment itself. The large proportion of workers out of employment for one month or more a year (20%) is striking evidence of this fact.

* 30% of the workers interviewed had just begun work or did not report on this point, so they have not been included in these figures.

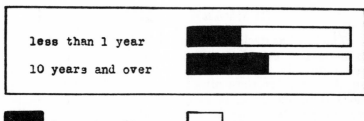

less than 1 year

10 years and over

■ less than $6   □ $6 or over

DIAGRAM 12.—Weekly Wages of Women Employed in Restaurants according to Length of Time in this Occupation.

LACK OF OPPORTUNITY IN RESTAURANT WORK.

Restaurant work is a "blind alley" trade. There is little opportunity for development or advancement. What training is necessary can be acquired in a few weeks, and the only position to which a girl can look forward is that of head waitress. There are no recognized degrees of skill in any part of the work connected with a restaurant. On the contrary, the tendency is in the direction of wearing girls out by overstrain rather than of giving them a chance. The girls who have been in the work the shortest time get higher pay than those who have been in it longest. Sixty-five per cent. of those who had been working less than a year were getting $6.00 or more a week, while only fifty-five per cent. of those who had been working over ten years were receiving as much. (See Diagram 12.) The woman who remains in restaurant work for more than a few years gradually loses her strength and ability, and can get a position only with an inferior type of restaurant, where the necessity for having a job forces her to accept whatever wage is offered her.

SUMMARY OF STUDY.

The law has declared illegal the employment of women in mercantile establishments longer than fifty-four hours or six days in any one week, on the ground that a working day of more than nine hours, or a working week of more than six days, is prejudicial to the health of the worker and therefore to the welfare of society. It has also declared illegal the employment of these women at night and it safeguards their interests further by insisting upon a definite period for the mid-day meal. Fifty-eight per cent. (58%) of the women employed in restaurants exceed the fifty-four hour limit, twenty per cent. (20%) work twelve hours a day and four per cent (4%) are employed at night. One-third do not have one day of rest in seven, and the majority are not allowed time off for their meals. Do not these women also need the protection of the law?

Restaurant work has much in common with work in mercantile establishments. Continuous standing and walking and the nervous strain entailed in serving many customers are features of both occupations. Besides this, restaurant work necessitates the lifting and carrying of heavy weights which may easily be disastrous not only to the worker herself, but to her children. Dr. Harris has expressly stated his belief that such work will injure the reproductive organs of a women unless she is guarded from overstrain. The larger proportion of restaurant workers are girls and young women, who are peculiarly susceptible to overstrain because of their youth.

There is abundant evidence from the testimony of the girls themselves that restaurant work is a severe tax and that the need for limiting hours of labor is strongly felt among them. Here are quoted a few of the remarks made by them, which could be duplicated many times:

"I think it's a shame to let a woman work twelve hours a day. I'm so tired at night I can't do anything but go to bed."

"I can't keep a job longer than four months because I get so nervous."

"This is my second week and I'm nearly dead, the hours are so long."

"It would be the grandest thing in the world if they could do away with the twelve-hour day."

27

To resist the unavoidable strain of the work, the restaurant worker must be in a normal, healthy state of mind and body. Our responsibility lies in seeing to it that conditions are such as to make this possible.

The results of fatigue do not end with the individual. It is common knowledge that health depends upon the power to resist disease. The person who has overworked is not only subject to the devastating action of fatigue poisons, but is a prey to any infections to which he may be exposed because he cannot throw them off. Working conditions which render large numbers of men and women susceptible to disease, and hence capable of spreading it, are a public menace. To allow such conditions to continue unchecked is inexcusable negligence.

These facts point directly to the crying need for the limitation of hours for women in restaurants, that the individual worker may be protected from overstrain, that the community may be guarded from the spread of contagious disease by people predisposed to infection through fatigue, and that the children of these women may be strong and capable of becoming useful citizens.

It must be conceded that the difficulty of regulating hours in restaurants is much greater than in mercantile establishments. Restaurants must be open for a longer period each day than any store needs to be or is likely to be. But the difficulties are not insuperable. By working the employees in shifts of nine consecutive hours a day and six days a week, and by replacing women by men for night duty, the most undesirable features of restaurant work would be abolished. Such a plan has already been tried successfully in a number of New York restaurants, proving that it is possible and feasible to regulate hours.

To limit by law the hours of labor for women employed in restaurants cannot be considered a new or revolutionary step. New York is already far behind the majority of other states in this respect. At the present time, twenty-seven states regulate the number of hours that women may work in restaurants, five having the eight-hour day.* Clearly, therefore, the establishment of a normal working day for this class of workers is not only reasonable, but, in the opinion of the greater number of states, it is essential to the best welfare of their people as a whole.

---

* See Appendix VI.

RECOMMENDATIONS FOR LEGISLATIVE AMENDMENT.

In view of the evidence brought to bear upon the subject, The Consumers' League wishes to urge the inclusion of women restaurant workers under the Mercantile Law, the general provisions of which are:

(1) That the working day shall not exceed nine (9) and the working week fifty-four (54) hours.

(2) That women shall not be employed between the hours of 10 p. m. and 7 a. m.

(3) That there shall be one day of rest in seven, and

(4) That there shall be a regular time off each day for meals.

APPENDIX I.

A STATEMENT FROM THE LABOR DEPARTMENT OF THE STATE OF NEW YORK ADVOCATING THE LIMITATION OF HOURS OF WORK FOR RESTAURANT EMPLOYEES.*

At present restaurant employees do not come within the provisions of the law relative to hours of labor of females, or the day of rest law. To the casual observer it is very evident that there is no other employment in which males and females are employed, where the hours of labor are so long, and where the employees are compelled to be constantly on their feet. It is admitted that there is no class of work in which so large a percentage of females is employed. The Legislature has recognized that the females working in restaurants should be protected to some extent, by providing in section 17 of the Labor Law that "Every person employing females—as waitresses in a hotel or restaurant shall provide and maintain suitable seats" but by the very nature of their work the employees have no opportunity to use these seats. There seems to be no good reason why the hours of employment of females in restaurants should not be subject to law as in mercantile establishments, and that all those employed in the same should enjoy the benefits of the day of rest law, as they do in other employments. The evil resulting from restaurants being exempt from the provisions of the Labor Law relating to hours and day of rest, is shown in the fact that bakeries and confectionery establishments have added to their business the serving of sandwiches and lunches, and endeavor to escape the provisions of the law by claiming that they are exempt because they are operating a restaurant. This illustrates the subterfuge to which many employers will resort rather than comply with the law.

JAMES L. GERNON,
Chief Mercantile Inspector.

---

* Annual Report of the Commissioner of Labor, 1914.

APPENDIX II.

EXTRACTS FROM A TENTATIVE REPORT ON THE PHYSICAL CONDITION OF WOMEN EMPLOYEES IN RESTAURANTS, BASED ON A STUDY CONDUCTED BY THE OCCUPATIONAL CLINIC OF THE HEALTH DEPARTMENT OF THE CITY OF NEW YORK.

From such opportunities for observation as our clinic study afforded us, it is safe to say that this occupation is one which may affect the health of women and in connection with long hours and small wages may combine to cause an increased existence of sickness among them. The effect of work that requires standing and running about while carrying loads for many hours during the day will be particularly marked upon the generative organs of the woman. The influence of the work in this particular, which we are unfortunately unable to study, because of the opposition it would inevitably arouse, leads me to believe that from this standpoint alone, there is a definite hazard to the child-bearing capacity of the woman. This is of vital consequence to society as a whole, as well as to the individual workers, and therefore well justifies every effort to correct the undesirable conditions that attend this occupation.

LOUIS I. HARRIS,
Chief, Division of Industrial Hygiene.

APPENDIX III.

RESTAURANT WORK FROM A WORKER'S POINT OF VIEW.

"A nine hour law would be a very good thing. I think long hours are very bad for women in restaurants. Most of them have varicose veins and flat feet, and a large number suffer from stomach trouble. Look at me, I am strong and healthy, but when I'm through at night, I am just all in. It's a dreadful nervous strain.

"Girls have to live on tips. If you tell the boss you can't make any, he says you are no good and discharges you. You have to put up with it or starve. The majority of girls—the better class of waitresses—if they could get a good living would be glad to do without tips. Of course it would be a revolution and would require a lot of agitation.

"Girls in restaurant work have greater temptations than most girls. Advances are always made, especially in certain districts. A great number go wrong because of so many advances.

"Nothing has ever been done for restaurant workers. The bosses all seem to think we are a lot of crooks. Waitresses think the same of them. Girls don't change their jobs so often because they like to. They get fired, mostly because the manager just wants to, or the work is too hard and the place miserable.

"There should be a nine-hour day, and two meals with half an hour allowed for each. Hours should be arranged consecutively. The best regulation would be to have girls work in shifts, going on at eight and coming off at five, or going on at eleven and working until eight. The same arrangement could be made for the kitchen help."

APPENDIX IV.

SCHEDULE USED.

NAME *Katie Penzel
ADDRESS 518 West 3rd St.
OCCUPATION Waitress

*Watkins 249 13th Ave. — CONJ. COND. V s. m. w. d.
Name of restaurant / Address
Counter: Tables Kind of restaurant
Y'RS AT WORK 5 this trade 18 mos. present firm 8½ tota..
Austria Birthplace
Austrian Nationality of father
Y'rs in U. S. 7 In N. Y.
Distance from work, car, walk, 30 min. time

AGE 26

LIVING COND. V
with family, boarding with relatives; friends, furnished room

REGULARITY OF WORK
Time idle in last 12 mo. due to slack season — Change of Work

V'ction with pay V without Ill Other NO Total 0
NO. MEALS A DAY AT REST. 3 Time off for meals NO

AVERAGE TIME IDLE DURING W'KING H'RS None

OTHER WORK REQUIRED IF NOT BUSY

ALLOWED TO LEAVE PROMPTLY

WHEN AND HOW OFTEN DOES OVERTIME WORK OCCUR

SUN. W'KED IN PAST YR 52 HOLIDAYS OFF IN PAST YR None TOTAL D'LY W'KLY

WAGES PER W'K $6. TIPS A W'K $3. OVERTIME PAY Total w'kly

FINES No

OTHER POSITION HELD NO

H'RS	FIRST WEEK		SECOND WEEK		OVERTIME WEEK	
	Begn.	Ed.	Total	Begn.	Ed.	Total	Begn.	Ed.	Total
MON.	8	8	12	8	8	12			
TUES.	8	8	12	8	8	12			
WED.	8	8	12	8	8	12			
THURS.	8	8	12	8	8	12			
FRI.	8	8	12	8	8	12			
SAT.	8	8	12	8	8	12			
SUN.	8	8	12	8	8	12			
TOTAL			84			84			

NO. TABLES RESP. FOR 14 Seat. cap. No. waited on a day 100 Distance from kitchen 70 ft. Hours W'g's per w'k
KIND OF SHOES WORN High heeled KIND OF FLOOR Wood No. trips to kitch. a day 200 Est. am't walked a day 5 miles
W'GHT OF TRAY Heavy

EFFECT ON HEALTH "Sore feet and a mean disposition."
DATE 2/23/'16 CITY N.Y.C. INVESTIGATOR M. E. N..... SOURCE OF INFORMATION Restaurant.

38

APPENDIX V.

TABLE 1.

Age of Women Employed in Restaurants, by Occupation.

Age	Waitresses		Cooks		Helpers		Total at each age	
	No.	Per Cent	No.	Per Cent	No.	Per Cent	No.	Per Cent
14 and under 16 years	2	.3	...	....	...	....	2	.2
16 and under 21 years	77	15.0	38	21.0	130	48.0	245	25.0
21 and under 30 years	288	55.0	54	29.4	87	32.0	429	44.0
30 and under 40 years	127	24.0	46	25.1	85	13.0	208	21.2
40 and under 50 years	25	4.7	37	20.2	15	5.3	77	8.0
50 and under 60 years	4	1.0	8	4.3	3	1.0	15	1.4
60 years and over.......	...	....	...	....	2	.7	2	.2
Total..........	523	100.00	183	100.00	272	100.00	978*	100.00

* Exclusive of 39 women who did not report on this point.

TABLE 2.

Age of Women Employed in Restaurants, by Nationality.

Nationality	14 and under 16 y'rs	16 and under 21 y'rs	21 and under 30 y'rs	30 and under 40 y'rs	40 and under 50 y'rs	50 and under 60 y'rs	60 y'rs and over	Total in each Nationality
American..........	..	48	156	81	26	3	..	314
Austro-Hungarian ..	1	155	137	55	18	4	..	370
Danish..............	..	..	4	..	1	..	..	5
Dutch	..	..	..	2	..	..	..	2
Eng. and Canadian.	..	..	16	12	1	2	..	31
French	..	..	1	1	2	1	..	5
German.......	1	6	36	20	12	1	..	76
Greek..............	..	1	..	..	..	..	..	1
Irish..............	..	3	27	22	11	3	2	68
Italian..	..	..	2	3	..	..	..	5
Polish	..	8	9	3	..	..	..	20
Russian............	..	19	14	1	2	1	..	37
Scandinavian.......	..	1	5	4	1	..	..	11
Scotch.............	..	..	1	1	..	..	..	2
Swiss	..	1	1	..	..	..	..	2
West Indian	..	..	2	3	..	..	..	5
Total..........	2	242	411	206	76	15	2	954*

* Exclusive of 63 women who did not report on this point.

TABLE 3.

Age of Women Employed in Restaurants, by Conjugal Condition.

Age	Single	Married	Widowed	Separated or Divorced	Total at each age
14 and under 16 years...	226	...	..	..	2
16 and under 21 years...	2	12	2	1	241
21 and under 30 years...	235	153	19	12	419
30 and under 40 years...	42	97	53	14	206
40 and under 50 years...	8	40	26	3	77
50 and under 60 years...	...	4	9	2	15
60 years and over	1	...	1	..	2
Total...............	514	306	110	32	962*

* Exclusive of 55 women who did not report on this point.

TABLE 4.

Age of Women Employed in Restaurants, by Living Condition.

| Age | Living with | | | | | Total at each age |
	Family	Relatives	Friends	Furnis'd Room	Proprie-tor	
14 and under 16 years	1	..	..	1	..	2
16 and under 21 years	82	78	59	18	6	243
21 and under 30 years	198	74	62	64	16	414
30 and under 40 years	92	37	24	36	10	199
40 and under 50 years	45	5	4	17	4	75
50 and under 60 years	11	2	..	1	..	14
60 years and over	...	..	..	2	..	2
Total...........	429	196	149	139	36	949*

* Exclusive of 68 women who did not report on this point.

TABLE 5.

Age of Women Employed in Restaurants, by Weekly Hours of Labor.

Weekly Hours of Labor	14 and under 16 y'rs	16 and under 21 y'rs	21 and under 30 y'rs	30 and under 40 y'rs	40 and under 50 y'rs	50 and under 60 y'rs	60 y'rs and over	Total in each hour group
54 hours and under...	2	77	193	109	27	6	1	415
55 and under 65 hours	..	67	85	22	12	3	..	189
65 and under 75 hours	..	47	76	32	15	1	..	171
75 and under 85 hours	..	41	58	34	14	4	1	152
85 and under 95 years	..	5	14	10	5	..	..	34
95 and under 105 years	..	5	3	..	2	1	..	11
105 years and over ...	..	3	..	1	2	..	..	6
Total	2	245	429	208	77	15	2	978*

* Exclusive of 39 women who did not report on this point.

TABLE 6.

Weekly Hours of Labor of Women Employed in Restaurants by Occupation.

Weekly Hours of Labor	Waitresses		Cooks		Helpers		Total in each hour group	
	No.	Per Cent	No.	Per Cent	No.	Per Cent	No.	Per Cent
Under 15 hours......	6	1.0	..	..	1	.3	7	.7
15 and under 25 h'rs..	75	14.0	1	.5	7	2.4	83	8.1
25 and under 35 h'rs..	89	16.2	1	.5	22	7.5	112	11.0
35 and under 45 h'rs..	45	8.2	7	4.0	13	4.5	65	6.3
45 and under 55 h'rs..	100	18.2	17	9.0	42	15.0	159	16.0
55 and under 65 h'rs..	78	14.2	34	18.0	85	30.1	197	19.3
65 and under 75 h'rs..	68	12.4	51	27.0	64	23.0	183	18.0
75 and under 85 h'rs..	73	13.3	49	26.0	36	13.0	158	15.5
85 and under 95 h'rs..	11	2.0	15	8.0	9	3.1	35	3.4
95 and under 105 h'rs.	2	.3	7	4.0	3	1.1	12	1.1
105 hours and over...	1	.2	5	3.0	..	..	6	.6
Total............	548	100.0	187	100.0	282	100.0	1017	100.0

TABLE 7.

Weekly Hours of Labor of Women Employed in Restaurants by Nationality.

Nationality	54 h'rs and under	55 and under 65 h'rs	65 and under 75 h'rs	75 and under 85 h'rs	85 and under 95 h'rs	95 and under 105 h's	105 h's and over	Total in each nationality
American.........	190	45	38	41	4	2	..	320
Austro-Hungarian.	83	88	97	81	18	6	6	379
Danish.............	5	..	..	..	..	..	..	5
Dutch.............	1	..	1	..	..	..	..	2
Eng. and Canadian	19	7	1	3	2	1	..	33
French...........	2	3	..	..	..	..	..	5
German...........	36	14	15	9	2	..	..	76
Greek............	1	..	..	..	..	..	..	1
Irish.............	44	5	7	12	1	1	..	70
Italian...........	3	1	1	1	..	..	..	6
Polish............	5	8	2	2	3	..	..	20
Russian...........	15	10	7	2	3	..	..	37
Scandinavian	6	2	..	1	..	2	..	11
Scotch	1	..	1	..	..	..	..	2
Swiss.............	1	..	..	1	..	..	..	2
West Indian.......	2	1	1	..	1	..	..	5
Total............	414	184	171	153	34	12	6	974*

*Exclusive of 43 women who did not report on this point.

TABLE 8.

Weekly Wages of Women Employed in Restaurants by Occupation.

Weekly Wage	Waitresses		Cooks		Helpers		Total in each wage group	
	No.	Per Cent	No.	Per Cent	No.	Per Cent	No.	Per Cent
Under $1............	1	.1	..	..	..	..	1	.1
$1 and under $2.....	1	.1	..	..	..	..	1	.1
2 and under 3.....	10	1.8	..	..	..	..	10	1.0
3 and under 4.....	74	14.0	1	.5	21	7.6	96	10.0
4 and under 5.....	107	20.2	4	2.1	19	7.0	130	13.2
5 and under 6.....	119	23.0	11	6.0	51	18.5	181	18.3
6 and under 7.....	107	20.2	15	8.1	119	43.4	241	25.0
7 and under 8.....	65	12.2	35	19.0	52	19.0	152	15.3
8 and under 9.....	26	5.0	36	20.0	7	2.5	69	6.0
9 and under 10.....	8	1.5	22	12.0	..	..	30	3.0
10 and over.........	10	1.9	60	32.3	5	2.0	75	8.0
Total	528	100.0	184	100.0	274	100.0	986*	100.0

* Exclusive of 31 women who did not report on this point.

TABLE 9.

Weekly Income of Women Employed in Restaurants by Occupation.

Weekly Income	Waitresses	Cooks	Helpers	Total
Under $1........................	2	..	..	2
$1 and under $2.................	2	..	..	2
2 and under 3.................	2	..	..	2
3 and under 4.................	16	1	21	38
4 and under 5.................	24	4	19	47
5 and under 6.................	47	11	51	109
6 and under 7.................	51	15	119	185
7 and under 8.................	61	35	52	148
8 and under 9.................	59	36	7	102
9 and under 10.................	60	22	..	82
10 and under 15................	129	51	5	185
15 and under 25................	73	9	..	82
25 and over	7	..	..	7
Total......................	533	184	274	991*

* Exclusive of 26 women who did not report on this point.

TABLE 10.

Wages of Women employed in Restaurants Showing Length of Time Idle during Preceding Year by Reason of Slack Season, Change of Work, Vacation with or Without Pay, Illnes or Other Causes.

Weekly Wage	No time idle	Under 2 weeks	2 weeks and under 1 month	1 month and under 2 months	2 months and under 3 months	3 months and under 4 months	4 months and under 5 months	5 months and under 6 months	6 months and over	Total in each wage group
Under $2	1									1
$2 and under $3	1	1	1	2	2					7
$3 and under $4	25	10	10	8	4	7	1	2	8	75
$4 and under $5	34	10	15	4	7	5	2	1	6	84
$5 and under $6	45	13	14	14	7	6	1	1	5	106
$6 and under $7	76	25	29	11	13	9		6	5	174
$7 and under $8	52	19	13	8	10	4	1		7	114
$8 and under $9	26	7	6	4	3	1		1	1	49
$9 and under $10	14	5	1	1	1		1	1		24
$10 and over	36	6	8	5		3	1		6	65
Total	310	96	97	57	47	35	7	12	38	699*

* Exclusive of 318 women who did not report on this point.

44

TABLE 11.

Weekly Wage of Women Employed in Restaurants by Nationality.

Nationality	Under $1	$1 and under $2	$2 and under $3	$3 and under $4	$4 and under $5	$5 and under $6	$6 and under $7	$7 and under $8	$8 and under $9	$9 and under $10	$10 and over	Total in each Nationality
American	1	1	6	45	49	78	54	35	16	7	15	307
Austro-Hungarian				22	24	40	115	70	34	20	47	372
Danish				2	1	1		1				5
Dutch						1	1					2
English and Canadian				4	10	7	6	1	3	1	1	32
French					1	1	1	2				5
German				11	14	10	13	15	2		8	74
Greek								1				1
Irish			2	6	19	13	18	8	3			69
Italian					1	1	3	1				6
Polish				1		3	6	9		1	3	20
Russian				1	1	9	15	2	5	1		37
Scandinavian					3	2		2	2			11
Scotch				1		1		1				2
Swiss						1						2
West Indian					1	1	2					4
Total	1	1	8	93	124	169	234	150	65	30	74	949*

* Exclusive of 68 women who did not report on this point.

45

APPENDIX VI.

STATES HAVING LAWS REGULATING WORK OF WOMEN EMPLOYED IN RESTAURANTS.

Hours

Hours in one day	Hours in one week	State
8	48	California
8	48	District of Columbia
8	56	Arizona
8	—	Colorado
8	—	Washington
9	54	Maine
9	54	Missouri
9	54	Nebraska
9	54	Texas
9	54	Utah
9	—	Idaho
9	—	Montana
9	—	Oklahoma*
10	54	Michigan
10	54	Ohio
10	54	Pennsylvania
10	55	Wisconsin
10	48	Wyoming
10	58	Minnesota
10	60	Kentucky
10	60	Louisiana
10	60	Mississippi
10	60	New Jersey
10	60	Oregon
10	—	Illinois
10½	55	New Hampshire†
10½	57	Tennessee

To be determined by Industrial Welfare Commission.

Arkansas
Kansas

* In cases of emergency 10 hours a day are allowed if not less than double for overtime is paid.

† Has an 8 and 48 hour law for night work

One Day of Rest in Seven Required

California*
District of Columbia
New Jersey
Pennsylvania

* Except in cases of emergency.

Night Work Forbidden

For all females
Nebraska

For females under 18
Arizona
California*
District of Columbia
Louisiana
New Hampshire

For females under 21
Ohio
Pennsylvania

Night Work Regulated

Not more than 48 hours in one week

For all females
New Hampshire
Wisconsin

* Except in cases of emergency.

Minimum Wage Required

Utah

To be determined by Industrial Welfare Commission

Arkansas
California
Colorado
Kansas
Massachusetts*
Minnesota*
Nebraska
Oregon
Washington
Wisconsin

* Not now in force—pending Supreme Court decision.

Meal Time Required

Arizona
Louisiana
Maine
Minnesota
New Hampshire
New Jersey
Ohio
Pennsylvania
Wisconsin
Wyoming

Seats Required

Arizona
Arkansas
California
District of Columbia
Idaho
Indiana
Kansas
Kentucky
Louisiana
Maine
Maryland
Michigan
Minnesota
Missouri
Montana
Nebraska
New York
North Carolina
Ohio
Oklahoma
Oregon
Pennsylvania
South Dakota
Texas
Utah
Vermont
Washington

Tips Forbidden

Arkansas
Iowa
Mississippi
South Carolina

BEHIND THE SCENES

IN A

HOTEL

PUBLISHED — FEBRUARY, 1922

BY

The Consumers' League of New York
289 FOURTH AVENUE
NEW YORK CITY

BEHIND THE SCENES IN A HOTEL

The modern hotel industry, claimed by the 35th Convention of the New York Hotel Association to be the fifth largest industry in the United States, is of compara-
Growth of the hotel industry tively recent growth. It is true that from the earliest times there have been inns and small hostels for the accommodation of the wayfarer. But this accommodation was the simple provision of board and lodging. The host and his family ran the house much as the modern boarding and rooming house is run. Until the late nineteenth century these houses, small and few in number, were usually at stage-coach changes along the road. With the great increase in travel, stimulated by the growth of steam railroads, hotels sprang up in great numbers and tended to concentrate in large centers of population. The invention of the elevator and the use of fireproof materials have made possible the construction of gigantic modern edifices. In the last few decades, under these conditions, more and more capital has been attracted to the industry until today there are 40,000 hotels, large and small, in the United States.

The individual hotel has developed into a complex institution, often of colossal size, supplying board and lodging on a most luxurious scale. In all parts of New York State, particularly in the smaller cities and towns, the small hotel with the inn tradition, with a simple table d'hôte service at one rate, still exists. But the tendency in New York City and in first and second class cities of the State has been toward a rapid expansion in the size of the individual establishment with an elaboration of service, and a specialization of hotel types. In the larger cities of the State, there are hotels with 450 or more rooms; in New York City there are many hotels with from 1000 to 2000 rooms. The largest hotel in New York, "the largest hotel in the world," by its own advertisement, contains 2200 rooms and 2200 baths. In answer to the special needs of special groups, different types of hotels have sprung up—the commercial-transient hotel which supplies complete, efficient but unelaborate service, the apartment house and family hotel with additional comforts and luxuries for residents of a longer period, the ultra-fashionable hotel, and the hotel that specializes in banquets, conventions and other social functions. No distinct classification holds, for there is usually an overlapping of types.

As the individual hotel has grown, hotel corporations and syndicates have developed. In New York City the largest, most complete hotels, almost without exception, are operated by hotel corporations. Two companies are each managing five of the largest hotels. Another company manages five hotels, two of which are in first class cities of New York State and three in other states. One company manages a group of fifteen smaller family hotels in New York City. Four hotels in four different up-state cities are managed by still another company. These corporation managers have united to form the New York State Hotel Men's Association and the Hotel Association of New York City for discussion of standards of operation. This exchange of opinion has resulted in the turning of hotel managers' thoughts to standards and policies in regard to labor, though as yet little of a concrete nature has been accomplished.

The labor force required to furnish service in the modern hotel has necessarily increased enormously since the day when **The labor force in the modern hotel** the host of the old-time hostel and his family personally cared for the needs of their guests. The following extract from a hotel manager's pamphlet on the running of big hotels gives some idea of the problems of labor management: "The operation of a single metropolitan hotel is too complex an undertaking to be likened to a gigantic piece of housekeeping. When it comes to running a group of six of the largest hotels in the world * * * the performance becomes of colossal size. The idea of employing 510 men just to cook food and another 925 just to wait on table, finding need at the same time to call in an average of 3000 waiters a month to help out on banquets, requiring 380 chambermaids to make beds and so on, must strike one pretty much as indicative of doing business on a wholesale scale."

Hotel managers, however, have been too prone to treat their business as housekeeping on a big scale. The transition from the small home industry with a few paying guests has been too rapid for adjustment to large scale method and standards. The attention of the hotel management, so far, has been directed toward standards of service to the public. It has only begun to think of standardization of conditions of employment for workers. It is perhaps the most backward and unregulated of industries from the point of view of wages, hours and living conditions, and comparable only with domestic service. It is one of the few industries which continues to house its employees as a part of the wage payment. It is one of the few industries in which tipping or the giving of gratuities to workers by the public persists.

There are inherent in the business certain definite obstacles to standardization of labor conditions. The most serious of these is that it is an almost continuous industry where work is carried on for eighteen of the twenty-four hours with peaks of greater volume throughout the day. The hotel managers, however, have not as yet put their best effort into solving this problem and to working out standardized conditions of employment.

Because for many years it has been aware of the long hours and living-in conditions in hotels, the Consumers' League of New York undertook a study of the **The reason for** hotel industry in the summer and fall **the investigation** of 1921 to discover the hours, wages, working and living conditions for women workers in the hotels of New York State.

The material used in the report was obtained by the investigators through their personal experience in working in typical women's jobs in the hotel indus- **The method used** try and by applying for work in a num- **in the investigation** ber of occupations in hotels and hotel employment offices. The material is necessarily incomplete and uneven though supplemented wherever possible by interviews with workers in the industry, officials and members of labor unions, employment agencies, etc. The report on wages, hours, and living-in conditions is a statement of the facts and conditions found in the hotels covered.

For the purpose of this investigation a hotel was defined, according to the American Travel and Hotel Directory, as "any building or structure of the better **The scope of the** class (whose minimum sized bedrooms **investigation** are at least 50¢ a night) used or maintained in whole or part for the entertainment of the traveling public or persons of temporary residence; with sleeping rooms furnished for hire with or without meals and (in order not to be confused with lodging or rooming house) maintaining an office or lobby register."

The scope of the investigation was necessarily limited because of the general condition of unemployment in other industries which turned many women to hotel work. The selection of hotels for the study, therefore, depended in a large measure upon the chance availability of jobs for the investigators. An attempt was made, however, to obtain work or apply for work in hotels as representative of the industry as possible. Hotels ranging in size from 25 to 2200 rooms were selected. The commercial hotel, the family apartment type, hotels featuring conventions and social functions—both transient and residential hotels were included. No resort or seasonal hotels were chosen.

It was found that the hotel industry centers in cities according to their size. The cities of New York State were classified according to population into first class cities of over 175,000; second class cities of from 50,000 to 175,000; and third class cities of less than 50,000 population. It proved to be far more difficult to secure employment in second and third class cities than in first class cities. In smaller centers this was in part due to the greater stability of the labor force and in the case of industrial cities to the unemployment situation. In cities of a few controlling industries, which had closed down, the hotel housekeepers invariably answered an inquiry for work with the statement that the works had shut down and so they had long waiting lists for all jobs.

The investigators applied for work in 96 hotels in New York State.

First class cities		47
Buffalo	12	
New York and Brooklyn	25	
Rochester	10	
Second class cities		28
Albany	7	
Binghamton	3	
Schenectady	4	
Syracuse	8	
Utica	6	
Third class cities		21
Elmira	2	
Hudson	2	
Ithaca	2	
Kingston	2	
Newburgh	3	
Troy	4	
Oswego	2	
Poughkeepsie	4	
Total		96

Work was secured in sixteen hotels, fourteen of which were in first class cities, one in Rochester, two in Buffalo, and eleven in New York and Brooklyn. One job was secured in Syracuse, a second class city, and one in Troy, a city of the third class.

It is impossible to give the exact percentage of women to men employed in hotels. A recent survey has been made, however, by the United States Bureau of **Occupations** Labor Statistics of hotels and restaurants **Covered** in 26 cities. This report shows that 40% of the employees in hotels and restaurants are women.* The percentage for hotels alone would undoubtedly be larger because men are usually employed as waiters

*United States Bureau of Labor Statistics. Wages of Hotel and Restaurant Employees. 1919. (Advance Release 486, Sept. 31, 1921.)

in the larger restaurants and in restaurants there is no large group of women chambermaids as in hotels.

Of the women in hotels, 56% are in the housekeeping department; 23% in the kitchen, dining room and pantry departments; and 20% in miscellaneous departments.* The miscellaneous departments comprise office employees, laundry workers, elevator, telephone and telegraph operators, seamstresses, wrap checkers and newsstand salesgirls. They have been excluded from this study on the ground that they are not typical of the hotel industry and may be studied under their respective occupations. Since newsstands and checking rooms are usually concessions, the investigators felt they could not be adequately dealt with but should be separately investigated.

More than half of the women workers in hotels are employed in the housekeeping department. 40.2% of the women in hotels are chambermaids, 10% cleaners or bathmaids, 2% linen room girls and 3.8% housekeepers.* Housekeepers have been excluded from this study because of the small percentage and the difficulty in securing information. The study of the housekeeping department, therefore, is confined to chambermaids, cleaners, bathmaids and linen room workers. The investigators worked in 14 jobs in the housekeeping department as chambermaid, bathmaid and linen room worker.

In the kitchen, cooks and assistant cooks are excluded on the ground of number. The information in the kitchen, dining room and pantry departments is, therefore, confined to waitresses and pantry workers. Two jobs were obtained in the kitchen as pantry worker. No work could be obtained as a waitress. All information regarding waitresses was secured from interviews with workers.

During the war the hotels of New York City found that advertisements, private fee-charging employment agencies and bulletins posted at the employees' entrance, were bringing in inadequate returns. The New York City Hotel Men's Association, therefore, opened its own free employment bureau, which served as a clearing house for all jobs open in

Labor Recruiting

---

*Minimum Wage Board of the District of Columbia. Wages of Women in Hotels and Restaurants. 1919. P. 10.

hotels belonging to the Association in New York City. One hotel company opened its own employment bureau to recruit workers for the five hotels under its management. This proved to be a temporary expedient only, to be used at a time when the hotels were in need of workers. When unemployment, due to the industrial depression, grew, the free employment bureaus were discontinued. This was at a time when the workers most needed them. The basis for the closing of the employment bureaus was voiced by one employment manager, "We don't need to do that now; we have a long line at the door every day for every job."

At present there is a return to the use of the advertisement and private employment agency. The old, unintelligent method of hiring the first worker in line after a casual interview, whether or not more suitable candidates may be available, is again the practice. In all but five of the hotels in which work was applied for the timekeeper and the head of the department interviewed the worker. It is true that some of the larger hotels in New York City under the control of big hotel corporations have developed employment departments. The employment managers have no labor policy, however. They are little more than clerks. They receive calls from the heads of departments and refer workers to them as they apply. No central record is kept. No job specifications have been worked out and no record is kept of the workers who leave. Even where there are employment managers the actual hiring is done by the heads of departments whose attitude is only too often, "These girls won't stay long anyway, so it doesn't much matter who is hired."

The following example illustrates how unintelligently an interview can be carried on by a housekeeper who was apparently an excellent manager of her department in other respects. The bad psychology and entire lack of employment technique in the interview is obvious. The interview took place in a first class hotel of a first class city in New York State. The girl waited for three-quarters of an hour outside the linen room. Finally, the housekeeper, a robust, emphatic person, came up the stairs. The girl took the initiative:

"Are you the housekeeper?"

"Yes," in a forbidding tone.

"Do you need any chambermaids?" She gave the girl an appraising look. She seemed to suspend judgment temporarily.

"Why, yes," she replied ungraciously, "I do need a steady girl. Are you a floater?"

"No, I'm not a floater," was the quick reply suggested to the girl. The housekeeper looked skeptical, but went on.

"Where've you worked?"

"—— in Albany."

"Oh," and she registered faint satisfaction, "that's the same management as this hotel," then, hardening again, "and did you get tired of that?"

"Oh, no," replied the candidate, quick to get her cue, "I liked it. I had to leave when we moved away from there." The housekeeper was mollified.

"You live here now?"

"Yes, I'm goin' to. I ain't got any people. I come from Lake George," showing she was a floater after all.

"You sure you ain't a floater and you'll come Sundays, every Sunday and take your night watches?" suggesting to the girl that she will expect her to be skipping Sunday and watches. "Well, wages is $10.50 a week, live out, hours 8-3 with night watch every 20th night from 6 to 11 P. M. When can you start?"

"Tomorrow."

"All right, now don't go back on me, will you?" implying that the girls usually do.

Then, as an afterthought, "What's your name?"

"Minnie ——, ma'am."

"All right, Minnie, 8 o'clock tomorrow. Now don't you go back on me, mind!"

Now that the hotels' employment agency is no longer open, a girl setting out to look for a job in a New York hotel first looks over the "Help

Getting a job in a hotel   Wanted" column in the New York World. There she may find advertisements such as these:

Wanted:

Chambermaid, with hotel experience, call before 10 A. M. Hotel ———; Live in.

Wanted:

Waitress, young girl, call before 10 A. M. Hotel ———.

Details are seldom given regarding wages or hours. If she is experienced she has a notion as to which are "good houses" so she rates the hotels in her mind and starts out early Monday morning to apply to them for a job.

Failing to find advertisements in the paper—and she does fail very often, for the labor supply in hotels is abundant— she makes the rounds of hotels, tipped off by a friend as to the best places to work. Or she joins the throng which files in and out of the hotel agencies on Sixth Avenue. The agency is usually on the second or third floor of a building with its sign in the doorway on the street floor. Under the sign are daily bulletin boards where the agency posts the "Jobs Open Today." On the one side are jobs for men, on the other jobs for women. The girl stops to pour over these with a motley crew of women, young and old, trim and slattern, of all nationalities.

"Pantry girl	$40 a month	Live in
Waitress	$30 a month	Live in
Chambermaid	$25 a month	Live in,"

she reads. If she finds anything to interest her, she ascends the several flights of dark stairs leading to the agency offices. She finds the employment agency divided into two parts, the men's department and the women's department. Behind a railing at one end is the interviewer of women, seated at a desk, talking to applicants one by one. In front of the railing in groups sit the candidates for jobs. There are neat waitresses, pretty Irish chambermaids, intelligent, mature pantry women, buxom Italian cooks, fat little bathmaids and cleaners, who are beginning to despair of getting a job anywhere. Conversation is animated and loud, often in brogue and broken English. It concerns disputes between house-keepers and maids, the awful hours and food in some hotels, the Irish question, prohibition, and how foreigners are taking girls' jobs.

Finally the interviewer turns and says, "Come on in. What are you looking for?" and she tells the candidate what jobs she has open and that she must obligate herself to pay the agency 10 per cent of her first month's salary if she gets a job through it. Then the girl gets a card from the interviewer directing her to a job. The employment office is not careful to conserve the worker's time or money. It is a commercial institution bent on profit. It sends her out to a hotel which wanted a chambermaid yesterday or early in the morning, without first telephoning to find out if the job is still open. It even "books" her for a job out-of-town with the most meager information regarding conditions in the hotel, although the worker is required to sign a contract to stay for a definite period of time. So she often finds herself, after visiting the agency, with a day lost, carfare lost and nothing gained, or a job secured which she finds it is impossible to keep because of some unknown disadvantages.

The hotel worker reflects, therefore, before going on a job recommended by the agency, deterred also by the 10 per cent fee. She will look around for herself and return here as a last resort. So she goes the round of the individual hotels again. When she reaches a hotel she walks to the rear hunting the employees' entrance. It is not hard to distinguish. It is indicated by an opening in the sidewalk and a steeply descending flight of iron steps, often circular, leading to the basement or second basement. These are often slippery and dark. They lead into an ill-lighted passage at the bottom, littered with storeroom supplies, old bottles, casks, bags of potatoes, etc. She has not made much progress before she is hailed by the timekeeper from his cage behind the time clock near the door.

"Hey, what do you want," he calls, "a job?" Sometimes he is scarcely so civil. She states her errand; she wants a job as a chambermaid, a waitress or a pantry girl, as the case may be. Sometimes she meets absolute discouragement from the timekeeper. Sometimes he is more good-natured and directs her to the housekeeper or the steward and shows her the way to the elevator. So she continues along the passage, dodging puddles and dripping pipes.

If she is a chambermaid, she goes to the housekeeper's office or the linen room. There she sits on a bench outside the door waiting audience along with other applying bathmaids and cleaners,—talking again about how awful it is to work in a hotel. When she does see the housekeeper, she is greeted with a roughly appraising look.

"Hotel experience?"

"Yes, ma'am."

"Where?" and "how long?"

But it is her appearance which counts, not her experience. If the candidate is young and nice looking, undeformed, and there is a job open, she will get it. If she is older and getting fat, all the experience in the world will do her no good. Her looks demote her to the bathmaid class and she will find it hard to get a job as that. So she is casual in giving her experience and she is casually hired. She doesn't learn much about the wages and hours or about the food and the room she is to have if she is to live in.

The girl decides to try it out for herself to see if it is "a good house for tips, how much you can pick up from the floor, what the watches are, how hard they work you, and what the grub and rooms are like." If she doesn't make out she'll leave—it doesn't much matter. She would do something else if she got half a chance—but she'll stick to this awhile anyway.

During the first few days in the hotel, she is shoved about and utterly lost. Perhaps no one even asks her name for several days. She doesn't know where **Learning the ways** her "station" or her "floor" is and how **of the hotel** much territory it covers. She doesn't know where the time clock is, where to get her meal ticket, where meals are served, where the toilets and dressing rooms are, where to get supplies and bed linen. She fumbles about "lost like" until she learns for herself. Sometimes she grows discouraged and leaves in the first few days. Sometimes she finds a friend who shows her around, takes her down to lunch, tells her what the rules are, and introduces her to her friends.

There were, of course, a few exceptions. In several cases rules and regulations were posted in linen closets and pantries and occasionally the housekeeper would put a new worker in charge of another girl to learn the rules. All hotels required the new worker to sign a contract stating that she would obey the rules of the establishment and would allow her baggage to be searched. The contracts seemed meaningless in that in most cases the workers had no way of knowing what the rules and regulations of the hotel were.

As for learning her job, "You're experienced, aren't you? Well, then, you know what to do," and the housekeeper dismisses all responsibility. The idea that **The training of** any woman knows how to do chamber **new employees** work or cleaning is prevalent in the housekeeping department. The girl is left to work alone, then scolded for her mistakes or even discharged without notice. One worker was turned out at 4 o'clock in the afternoon with no money and another girl put in her bed that night because the housekeeper "didn't like the way she swept." In a few exceptional cases the housekeeper taught the new girls by the "you watch me" method.

The failure of hotels to train their employees was pointed out by the United States Federal Board of Vocational Education which had been requested by the American Hotel Association to make an investigation of the possibilities for vocational training in the industry. The report points out that the hotel industry has developed so fast from a home industry that managers have not perfected their organization. Department heads have not been instructed that one of their functions is the training of new workers. The report stresses the fact that training must be based on a clear definition of jobs and that jobs have not yet been analyzed by the management. "As hotel men pay more attention to training and promotion of deserving employees, there will be greater inducement to capable young people to enter the business. Such opportunities for training and promotion will also lessen the turnover of labor and consequently lessen the cost of operation."* In New York State there seems little indication that hotels have profited by this report.

There was no such thing as a transfer or promotion policy in hotels where work was obtained. The nearest approach to it was found in one hotel where in the **Transfers and** housekeeping department women were some- **Promotion** times taken on as bathmaids at $25 a month and later became chambermaids at $28 a month. There their advancement ceased. Some hotels have rules that no chambermaids may be promoted to linen room workers. There was no cooperation between departments in transferring workers from one department to another.

*L. S. Hawkins, representing the Federal Board of Vocational Education. Vocational Education in the Hotel Business, A Report to the American Hotel Association of the United States and Canada. P. 10.

HOURS

One of the most important conditions of work to the woman hotel employee is the number and distribution of the hours she works. As the hotel industry is a continuous one, most departments operate 18 out of the 24 hours. Within these 18 hours, as has already been pointed out, there are peaks of work when a larger force is necessary. Broken shifts and long and short working days are the result. The working days are made even more irregular by lack of regular lunch periods and regular closing time for those workers who live in in the hotel.

The length and distribution of hours is so different for the different departments that it is necessary to discuss the housekeeping department and the kitchen, pantry and dining room departments separately.

Housekeeping Department

The function of the housekeeping department in a hotel is the housing of guests. It has sole charge of the bedroom floors. The function of the women workers in this department is to clean the bedrooms and corridors, to change the linen on the beds, to dust and sweep, supply fresh towels and soap and care for the baths, private and public. The bulk of this work falls in the daylight hours when guests have risen and gone about their business. In the large transient hotels, however, guests are coming into the hotel and leaving it until midnight. Part of the workers must, therefore, be on hand to attend to the incidental wants of the guests and make up new rooms at night.

The women employed in greatest numbers in the housekeeping department are the chambermaids, who clean rooms and make the beds, the bathmaids, who clean and scrub out the bathrooms and corridors and the special cleaners. Of these, the bathmaids' and cleaners' work falls in fairly regular shifts. Bathmaids work a day shift and cleaners, in the big hotels, work a day and a night shift. Chambermaids, on the other hand, have night work distributed among them according to the needs of the establishment.

The work of the bathmaids and the cleaners is, perhaps, the hardest women have to do in hotels. All day long they scrub out wash basins, tubs and toilets, **Bathmaids' and** polish brass, and mop up floors on **cleaners' hours** their hands and knees. Their work is of fairly uniform intensity. It is "humiliating work," as one bathmaid said, and for this reason the higher type of maid refuses to take it. The hours of the bathmaids are, however, the best in the housekeeping department. This has led some chambermaids in spite of prejudice against the work to prefer bathmaids' jobs. In thirteen hotels in which work was obtained in the housekeeping department bathmaids worked a nine-hour day or less. The hours of work fell between 7.30 and 5 o'clock. In two hotels, they worked 8½-hour days, 7 hotels a 7½-hour day, in 3 hotels a 7-hour day and in one hotel a 6½-hour day.* Lunch periods were unstandardized, as most of the bathmaids ate in the hotels.

The special cleaners worked the same daily hours as bathmaids. In some hotels there was a squad of night cleaners also who worked from 6 P. M. to 12 midnight, and in the largest hotels there was another shift working from 12 midnight until 7 A. M. No information could be secured concerning these night shifts.

The weekly hours for bathmaids in the hotels varied from 45 to 54 hours. In five of the nine hotels for which weekly hours were obtained bathmaids were required to work from 45 to 50 hours a week and in four hotels from 50 to 54 hours a week. The weekly hours for bathmaids are long in spite of a fairly short working day because they work a seven-day week. The Sunday hours are shorter than hours for week days, varying from 5½ to 7 hours. Sunday work for bathmaids seems unnecessary. The guests stay in their rooms late Sunday morning and do not wish to be disturbed by cleaning. Bathmaids are used to clean outmaids' closets and corridors and to take the places of the chambermaids who have failed to report for Sunday work. Because they have no regular

---

*The hours given are exclusive of the lunch period. One-half hour has been deducted in computing the daily hour schedules.

work to do on Sunday, bathmaids highly resent the imposition of Sunday work. As their work is of an especially fatiguing nature they believe they are entitled to one day of rest. "It's mean to call you in on Sunday and keep you sitting around when you might be home resting or off having a good time," they would say. In three of the hotels bathmaids were given two days off a month or every other Sunday.

The large majority of workers in the housekeeping department are chambermaids. The hours of work for chambermaids are the most unstandardized

Chambermaids' Hours
of those of any occupation in the hotel. They vary greatly from establishment to establishment. Different maids in the same hotel work different hours, and hours differ for each maid on successive days of the week. This has made it difficult to give a general statement of the working hours of chambermaids.

In transient hotels chambermaids work a daily shift in which they change the linen, dust, and sweep in an assigned number of rooms. This work falls within a fairly regular period. In addition they take turns at being on watch in the morning from 7 o'clock to 8, in the afternoon from 4 to 6 o'clock, and at night from 6 to 12 o'clock, or 6 to 10, according to the establishment. Maids have an irregular lunch period also, except a small minority in a few hotels who were found to take an hour and go home. The workers leave the floor in many hotels when they have finished their daily work often several hours earlier than the leaving time scheduled. On the other hand, they are often kept beyond the scheduled leaving hour because there is a shortage of linen and they must wait for it in order to make up their rooms.

Extra shifts or watches occur in frequencies of from one watch every twentieth night to one watch every morning, afternoon or evening. In two hotels no night watch for the regular chambermaids occurred. A relief watch of maids was added to the staff to work from 6 to 12 o'clock. In one of the hotels this was installed as an economy measure. In several other hotels night watches were made optional and extra pay was received by a maid for each watch taken. Under this system some maids, in order to increase their earnings, might overtax their strength. Night watch in the smaller cities lasted only until 10 o'clock and occurred at less frequent intervals.

When a girl complains of long hours, the housekeeper usually replies that there is a nice short day on Sunday. The maids do not take this as a great consolation, for they regard one full day's rest in seven as their right. In all but two hotels in which jobs were held, a straight seven-day week was worked by all chambermaids. The Sunday hours were shorter, workers usually leaving at 2 P. M. instead of 4 P. M. In the other two hotels two days off each month were allowed. These days off were most irregularly given, however, at the discretion of the housekeeper. If there was a shortage of maids, there were no days off. One worker in one of these hotels said she had been there two months and had worked every day.

In 12 of the 14 hotels* in which jobs were obtained as chambermaids the regular daily shift varied from 6½ hours to 8½ hours, exclusive of the lunch period. The regular weekly shifts varied from 45½ to 59½ hours. *But the extra shifts make the weekly hours worked by chambermaids excessively long.* The average number of hours worked weekly in "extra watches" varied from none to 21.04 hours. The actual working hours for chambermaids, by which is meant the regular weekly hours plus the average number of extra hours each week, in the 12 hotels, are as follows:

49.38	54.50
50.16	56.70
50.75	59.27
50.94	60.90
52.50	66.54
52.50	70.03

In no case is a 48-hour week found, and it can be seen that in over half of the hotels chambermaids worked more than 54 hours.

---

*Two hotels have been omitted from the analysis of hours because of inadequate information on extra shifts.

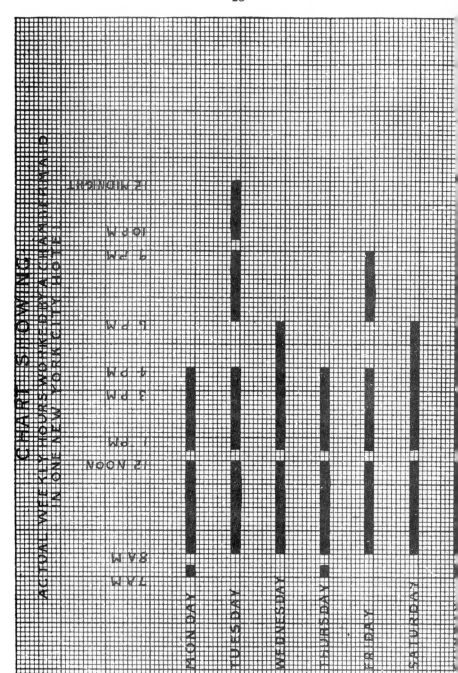

The chart on the opposite page shows the weekly hours actually worked by chambermaids in one sample hotel in New York City. Beside her regular hours the chambermaid had the morning watch from 7 to 8 A. M., with time allowed for her to run down and eat her breakfast. The second day there was a long watch from 6 P. M. to 12 P. M., the following day a short afternoon watch from 4 to 6 P. M., and every third afternoon after four o'clock she had to herself.

Linen room workers worked a long and short day. They usually reported at 8 o'clock and worked until 11 or 12 o'clock one day. They were then off **Hours of linen room workers** until 6 and worked until 12 midnight. The next day they worked from 12 noon to 6 P. M.

In all hotels where "extra watches" were worked the maids felt the strain of the excessive hours. On days on which an extra watch from 6 to 12 was **Physical effects of ex-** worked, a maid was on her feet **cessive hours of work** from 8 to 4, then with two hours' respite from 6 to 12, or 14 hours a day, with short intervals off for meals. She came to her work the next day with dragging step and a listless air, complaining that she never got rested. Her habits of life were disturbed by the irregularity of hours for succeeding days. She snatched sleep when she could. After work maids always went to their rooms to rest until supper time. Workers living out frequently kept beds in the hotel on which to snatch sleep. The work is indoors in an overheated hotel. Excessive hours prevent the maids from getting sufficient exercise in the fresh air. It is impossible to keep in good physical condition under such working conditions. The maids age prematurely. "Oh, you think I am an old woman. I am only thirty. You'll look like me, too, if you stay here long." Similar statements were made by several of the maids. The bathmaids particularly were a jaded and fatigued group of women workers. The older ones in New York City were bent from constant stooping. Even strong, young Polish girls, who were frequently found working as bathmaids in up-state cities, were so tired out at night that they spent their evenings lying on their beds.

The complaint of maids regarding hours of work was general. In several hotels there had been an organized protest to the manager against a seven-day week. In one hotel, with the help of a union, maids were organized and the night watch was abolished. For the most part, however, complaint took the form of individual grumbling, dissatisfaction, and changing of jobs. One worker greeted a new worker as she came into her bedroom sick after a night watch on a very hot night, "They work you like dogs here, you better not stay." "I was so tired last night I could have cried," said another worker. "My feet were all swollen this morning. These night watches will kill me yet." Many complained of sore feet and varicose veins from continual standing. Of the seven-day week, one young maid said, "You don't mind so much in the winter time, but in the summer to see everybody going off to the country and you working all day indoors in a hot, stuffy hotel, with never a day to go anywhere or see your family—it's terrible."

The hotel which installed a relief night shift for chambermaids as an economy measure, was wise. After observing the overtired, listless maids skimp their work the day following a long night watch, one cannot but conclude that long hours of work for women are a bad business policy. The tired worker not only does poor work herself, but she demoralizes the other more alert workers on the force. "Just make up the beds with the sheets that's on 'em. Those people aren't going out today anyway. Give the rooms a lick and a promise, I say. I'm tired today," is often heard while the maids are eating lunch. A feeling of resentment against long hours tends to make the workers dissatisfied and careless about their work. All feeling of responsibility for good work is diminished accordingly.

Effect of long hours on efficiency

In order to mollify maids, housekeepers allow them to leave their stations as soon as they have covered the work on their daily shift. This makes for hastily finished work and a further unstandardized day. It means that, instead of all maids getting a regular number of hours off duty, clever and unscrupulous individuals steal time at the expense of others. The effect of long hours on attendance is marked. Maids frequently take days off without pay. Some make a practice of turning up for Sunday work several times a month only. And after the continued strain of some months of night watches and seven-day week work, maids feel they "need a vacation and a change" and leave their jobs.

Maids who live in a hotel go out little unless they are very young. After working hours they lie on their beds and sleep or gossip. When they do leave the hotel it is either to go to mass or to find some exciting form of amusement. The younger girls made "dates" casually with guests and other men to go to the movies and Coney Island. Girls who are more backward had often been nowhere outside the hotel, except to church. A Danish girl, who was working in a large New York City hotel, said she knew no one in New York City and had not been anywhere except to go to church with another maid one Sunday and she wouldn't go there again because they all laughed at her when she took off her hat. She said she was too tired to go to the movies at night because these night watches were "fierce"—she was just tired all the time. She worked in one of the hotels which had an extra watch every day. Another worker, a young Polish bathmaid, complained, "I am too tired to ever go home and see my people any more at night. I used to go every other night and I get awful lonesome for them now, but I just can't get cleaned up and dress." This girl was sixteen and had been working as a bathmaid for three months. Another young bathmaid said, "I am too tired to ever go to dances. I just want to rest at night. I can't stand it anyway, it's too hard."

Effect of long hours on recreation

Dining-Room, Kitchen and Pantry Departments

The work of the waitress in a hotel reaches its peak at meal hours and slackens between times. For this reason waitresses work "broken shifts." The daily and **Waitresses' Hours** weekly hours of the waitresses interviewed were not as unstandardized or as excessive in length as hours for chambermaids. They worked a six-day week in all cases. But the distribution of hours of work in broken shifts caused great inconvenience to the workers. Those who lived in were apathetic but those who lived out and wished to return home after hours of work complained bitterly. If the worker lives any distance from the hotel it is impossible for her to change her clothes twice, allow time for street car ride, and return to work in the rest period allowed between the morning and the evening shift. There is, besides, the expense of extra carfare to be considered.

In one New York City hotel, according to a woman worker's statement, she reported for work at 11 A. M. and worked till 4 P. M. She then left her station for 1½ hours' rest and returned at 5.30 to work until 9 P. M. She ate her meals and changed her clothes upon her own time. She complained that she could not go home in the afternoon because she lived too far away to change to street clothes twice and allow for car rides. The hotel had a rest room where she stayed for the 1½-hour rest period. "Of course," she said, "it is wasted time." She worked no overtime, but the work was heavy during the hours in which she worked so that she was often too tired and nervous to eat her meals.

In another hotel a worker stated that she worked broken shifts one week in the day time and straight shifts the next week when she was on night work. One week she worked from 6 A. M. to 11 A. M., had a rest period from 11 A. M. to 6 P. M., and worked 6 P. M. to 9 P. M. The next week she worked from 5.30 P. M. until 12 P. M. She ate her meals on her own time, but changed her clothes on working time. Overtime varied from 1 to 1½ hours a day.

In the third hotel for which information was secured the

waitresses lived in. The work was divided into three shifts; from 6.30 A. M. to 8.30 A. M., from 10.30 A. M. to 2.30 P. M., and from 5.30 P. M. to 7.30 P. M. This makes an 8-hour day if only the hours actually worked are counted in.

In the kitchen and pantry the hours range from 8 to 9 daily with a six-day week. Here again the broken shifts and the long and short day were found. In the two hotels where **Hours of pantry maids** jobs were obtained in the kitchens **and kitchen help** and pantries, there were two groups of women dishwashers, a day shift and a night shift. The day shift worked from 7 A. M. to 4 P. M., or an 8½-hour day, exclusive of ½ hour for lunch. The night shift worked from 4 P. M. to 1 A. M., or an 8½-hour day. They worked six days, or a 51-hour week.

The other workers in the pantry and kitchen of one of these hotels worked broken shifts. The workers had rotating shifts with a long day and then a short day. On the day before the weekly day off, each worker worked a 12 or 13-hour day. The irregularity of a pantry worker's hours and the distribution over a seven-day period, is shown on the chart on the following page. The length of working hours for the worker in this instance ranged from 6 to 13 hours daily. On days on which the long shift was worked, the hours were distributed over a period of 18 hours. The total weekly hours of this pantry worker were 63. The two other pantry workers in this hotel worked a 56-hour week and a 60-hour week, respectively. Since a girl always worked a long day of 12 to 13 hours before her free day, she was unable to derive full benefit from it because of fatigue.

As the other hotel in which a pantry job was held was much larger, pantry and kitchen work was more specialized. There were pantry maids, coffee women, butter and cream women, and vegetable women. The butter and cream women and the pantry maids (salad girls) had the most irregular shifts. Two pantry maids worked a straight shift from 7 A. M. to 4 P. M. or a 9-hour day; two worked broken shifts from 8 A. M. to 2 P. M. and from 6 P. M. to 8 P. M., or an 8-

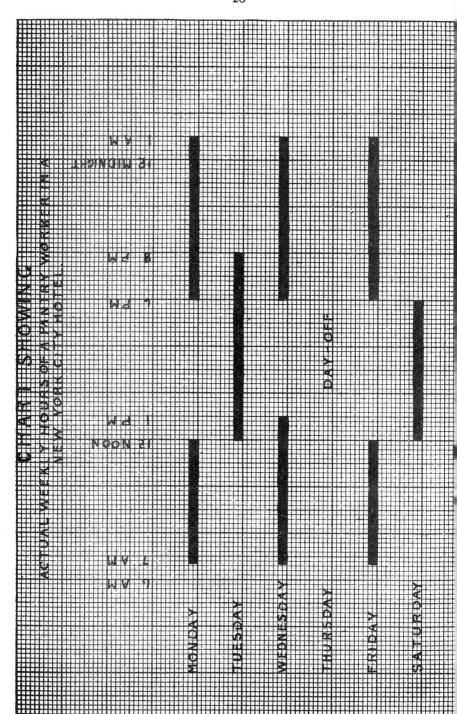

CHART SHOWING

ACTUAL WEEKLY HOURS OF A PANTRY WORKER IN A
NEW YORK CITY HOTEL

hour day; and one worked from 4 P. M. to 1 A. M., a 9-hour day. These women ate their meals on the job so no time has been deducted for lunch hours.

Broken shifts distributed over a long period of time with scheduled hours of work changing from day to day are a great hardship to the woman **The effect of broken** worker. Aside from the fact that **and irregular shifts on** two hours in the middle of the **the worker** afternoon are useless to a woman if she must dress and take a car to go home, and take a car to return and dress again on reaching the hotel, broken shifts mean that meals and sleep must be snatched at irregular intervals. Such a hit or miss existence, with no regular hours for work, rest and recreation, does not make for the physical well-being of the worker.

WAGES

When taking a position in a hotel the woman worker bargains as an individual for the wages she is to receive. She is without the support of a labor organization which would have set a standard for her occupation and would assist her in maintaining it. She applies for work in an industry where the wage scales are determined largely by the inclination of the hotel managers and by the labor supply. She must go from hotel to hotel to learn what is being paid, for the wage opportunities vary from establishment to establishment.

She cannot even estimate the value of the wage she is to receive in the majority of jobs. This is due to two uncertain elements in the earnings of hotel workers; tipping and compensation other than money in the form of board and room. Because she is not in a position to gauge the amount of the tips she will receive and the quality of the board and lodging, the only recourse of the applicant is to try out the job for a time. "Well, I'll try it out for a week and see how I make out," is the common expression of the new worker. If it is not a good house for tips, if she can't eat the food, and if the living-in conditions are unbearable, she will go somewhere else and try again. By trying out job after job she loses time and greatly decreases her yearly earnings.

Cash Wages

In the smaller hotels of New York City and the hotels of the smaller cities of the State, a straight cash wage was paid to women workers in all occupations. The wages of chambermaids and bathmaids varied from $8.77 a week to $16 in the 46 hotels where wage rates were obtained. Of these, the one hotel paying $8.77 a week was the largest hotel of a second class city where two large factories employing great numbers of women had closed down. The housekeeper said, "The works have shut down, so you can get workers at any price." The one hotel paying $16 a week employed only three maids on a long-hour schedule.

Wages when the workers live out

The straight cash wages paid to chambermaids and bath-maids in the 46 hotels are as follows:

1	paid at least	$ 8	but less than	$ 9	per week
9	" " "	9	" " "	10	" "
11	" " "	10	" " "	11	" "
9	" " "	11	" " "	12	" "
11	" " "	12	" " "	13	" "
2	" " "	13	" " "	14	" "
2	" " "	14	" " "	15	" "
0	" " "	15	" " "	16	" "
1*	" " "	16	" " "	17	" "

Few women workers were employed in the kitchens and pantries of these hotels. No waitresses were employed.

A comparison of these wage rates may be made with the minimum wage fixed for hotel workers in 1919 in the District of Columbia where the cost of living is comparable to that of New York State. The Minimum Wage Board of the District of Columbia decided that a wage of $16.50 a week was the minimum on which a self-supporting woman could live. In no case do the hotels investigated in New York State pay this minimum when a straight cash wage is paid and the workers do not live in the hotels. It can be seen from these figures that 40 of the 46 hotels pay between $9 and $13 or an average of $11 per week.

In six hotels at which jobs were applied for, lodging was offered, but no meals. The fol-
Wages including lodging lowing cash wages were offered
but no meals to chambermaids and bathmaids in addition to lodging:

1	paid at least	$ 8	but less than	$ 9	per week
3	" " "	9	" " "	10	" "
1	" " "	10	" " "	11	" "
1	" " "	11	" " "	12	" "

No information was obtained for pantry workers or waitresses in this group.

---

*The actual wage paid in this group was $16.00.

The Minimum Wage Board of the District of Columbia, in extending its minimum wage of $16.50 to hotel workers who were living-in, attempted to set a money value on the board and lodging furnished by the hotel. Because there was no way of determining its actual cost to the hotel management, the minimum cost of room and board for a self-supporting woman in the District of Columbia was taken. The figure used is $9 a week for board and lodging; two-thirds or $6 for board, and one-third or $3 for lodging.* $13.50 is, therefore, the minimum on which a woman can maintain herself while living-in in a hotel but taking her meals outside. None of the hotels in New York State, furnishing lodging in addition to a cash wage, paid this minimum.

In 8 hotels which paid the workers their wage, plus three meals a day, the following cash wages were paid to chambermaids and bathmaids:

Wages including three meals and no lodging

1	paid at least	$ 6	but less than	$ 7 per week
0	" " "	7	" " "	8 " "
1	" " "	8	" " "	9 " "
5	" " "	9	" " "	10 " "
1**	" " "	10	" " "	11 " "

No information was obtained for pantry workers or waitresses in this group.

If the $16.50 minimum wage of the District of Columbia is taken, and $6 to cover the cost of three meals deducted, the minimum wage for this group would be $10.50. In no case was this amount received.

The largest New York City hotels and the largest hotels

---

*Minimum Wage Board of the District of Columbia. Wages of Women in Hotels and Restaurants in the District of Columbia. P. 16.

**The actual wage paid in this group was $10.00.

in first class cities require maids to live in and prefer that some of the pantry workers and waitresses should do so. In these hotels chambermaids and bath-maids living-in have the following wage rates:

Wages including board and lodging

1	paid at least $	4	but less than $	5	per week
7	" " "	5	" " "	6	" "
17	" " "	6	" " "	7	" "
1	" " "	7	" " "	8	" "
2	" " "	8	" " "	9	" "
1	" " "	9	" " "	10	" "

If $9 for board and lodging is deducted from the $16.50 minimum wage of the District of Columbia, $7.50 is left as the minimum wage for this group of workers. When the wages of chambermaids living-in are taken, it will be noted that only four out of twenty-nine hotels pay this wage or more, and that over half pay between $6 and $7 per week.

Waitresses in one hotel in New York City where board and room are furnished received $6.92 a week. Pantry workers, who are a skilled class, received one of the highest wage rates found for women workers in hotels. They have, however, no access to tips. In one hotel they received $50 a month with board and lodging, or $11.53 a week, and in another hotel $55 a month with board and lodging, or $12.29 a week. In two hotels kitchen workers received $30 a month whether they lived in or out.

Tipping

Tips, or the giving of gratuities by the patrons of the hotel to workers who serve them, is the most unstandardized part of the earnings of the worker. Because the giving of tips depends not only on the whim of the public but upon the general prosperity of the country and the individual prosperity of the patron, it admits of no standardization. Tipping seems incongruous in that, by its own definition, the function of the hotel is service. It amounts to a direct payment by the public of a part of the worker's wage.

It should be remembered that tips are received by chambermaids and waitresses only. There are large numbers of bathmaids, cleaners, pantry and kitchen help who have no access to tips.

The practice of tipping is defended by both workers and managers, although it operates to the disadvantage of both.

The disadvantages of tipping

The management defends tipping on the ground that the public wishes to tip. "He feels the servant has given something extra and unexpected and he wants to pay something for it—he tips."* This manager indirectly admits, however, that tipping is an imposition on the patron when he assures his guests that no discourtesy will be shown a guest who does not tip. If managers were candid they might admit that they wish the public to tip because it enables them to pay their employees a lower wage rate.

Patrons are frequently annoyed by the persistency of workers in procuring tips. The guest who tips will get service at the expense of the guest who doesn't—maids are frank to admit this—and there is consequently dissatisfaction of one class of guests. A guest in a hotel has come to feel that the hotel rate is but one item in the expense of staying there and naturally he resents it.

Between the workers and their superiors disputes arise over the distribution of tips. Dissatisfaction and lack of cooperation result which obstruct the smooth functioning of departments. Chambermaids designate desk clerks as "sneaking devils," because they think the desk clerk takes their tips. They hate the bell-boys because they think they get more than their share of tips. Waitresses, especially banquet waitresses, have a constant grudge against head waiters. They think they hold back a large share of tips from them. Maids resent it when housekeepers give them transient cor-

*Statler Service Codes. P. 7.

ridors where tips are poor, and waitresses accuse head waiters of putting them on poor stations.

Tips are a disadvantage to the worker because she can never know what her weekly earnings are to be and plan her expenses accordingly. But she defends tipping because she feels that this is the only part of her earnings over which she has control. She knows her wage rate will be low, but she may get big tips through her own efforts. The uncertainty of the amount of tips has a romantic fascination for the maid or waitress. She thinks that by an ingratiating manner to the guest, by staying overtime to be on the spot when a guest leaves, by her persistence, and by chance of securing a good floor or station she will get tipped. Moreover, she has heard many stories of good tips. Maids and waitresses boast of the good tips they receive and remain silent when they get none. Each maid hopes that she will be the lucky one. But she comes to realize reluctantly that she cannot control tips. She may not get a good floor if she is a chambermaid but one on which transients stop for one night and are never seen. In modern hotels the "regulars" stop on the higher floors. She may not obtain favor with the housekeeper or the desk clerk or the head waiter. She may be at lunch or supper when a guest leaves. She may be growing old and the guest will not be pleased by her manner. The lot of the older chambermaid who is in many respects more efficient than the younger one, is especially hard. She does not get tips and she ceases to expect them. This discrimination against the experienced worker illustrates the unfairness of tips as a part of the workers' wage. Tips depend not so much on service as on a pleasing appearance and manner. Advice to a new maid is to "fix yourself up" and "don't be bashful. The ones who get tips are those who stick around and sass 'em back and make them notice you." There is a question as to how many of the tips received are legitimate tips. The danger to a young girl, who ingratiates herself with the guests to get tips, is only too evident. The girls often said to those who got no tips, "Oh, you're too straight to make good tips. Make up to them."

The dissatisfaction of the maid who gets low tips grows and finally she leaves her job. An employment manager of a large group of hotels in New York City said, "From my experience as employment manager, I am thoroughly convinced that the tipping system is more directly responsible for labor turnover in hotels than any other one thing. An employee will leave one hotel to go to another where exactly the same wages are paid if she thinks the chance for tips is better."

Tipping, as a factor in the workers' earnings, has been generally overestimated. A study, made by the United States Bureau of Labor Statistics during the war period when tipping was comparatively high, shows that the average tip for a chambermaid in Buffalo was 40¢ a day and the highest was only 71¢. In New York City the average tip received by the chambermaids was 49¢ and the highest tip 83¢.* The Minimum Wage Board of the District of Columbia in 1919 says of tipping: "Of the 48 maids from whom data on this point were obtained, 8 stated that they received no tips, 7 stated the amount to be very little and the average for those giving actual figures was $1.22 per week. It seems evident that the tips received by maids were not sufficient to make any appreciable addition to their wages."**

The relation of tipping to wages

Certainly in New York State, according to the data gathered from this investigation, tipping for chambermaids is negligible. It is difficult to get an accurate estimate from maids as to their average weekly tips. They remember a $5 tip they once got but not how much they get each week. In one of the largest New York hotels, one maid says she gets $5 once in a while, then nothing for weeks at a time. One had had $3 in the three months she had worked in the hotel. Another made 50 cents in 5 days. The investigators, while working in hotels, received less than $1 a week in New York City hotels and in the other hotels of New York State only an occasional small tip of from 15 to 25 cents. It may have been due in part to the fact that as new maids they worked

---

*Monthly Labor Review, September 1919. Wages and Hours of Hotel and Restaurant Employees. P. 193.

**Minimum Wage Board of the District of Columbia. Wages of Women in Hotels and Restaurants. 1919. P. 5.

on corridors for transients and not for permanent guests. Their experience, however, was borne out by statements of other maids. There was constant complaint that tips were low. In up-state cities maids said, "You never expect tips from travelling men any more. Only when a play actress or somebody like that comes from New York you get a tip." In New York City also there was complaint that "houses are no good for tips now" and "no rich people come any more."

Waitresses, the few whom it was possible to interview, received much larger tips than maids. It is more customary to tip waitresses and they are always on the spot to receive their tips. Waitresses interviewed received from $3 to $5 a day in tips. They form, however, a minority of women hotel workers and their position in the industry is precarious, due to the antagonism of the men waiters.

That a hotel can be run without tips has been demonstrated by a women's hotel in Washington, D. C., in which a minimum wage of $16.50 is paid. A group of restaurants in New York City realizing the unfairness of the tipping system, has attempted a standardization of tips. The patron pays a 10% service charge with his bill, which per cent goes to the waiter at the end of the week. This seems entirely satisfactory to the worker in that it makes for a certainty of tips, but the pernicious principle underlying the tipping system persists.

Living-in

The other uncertain element in a woman hotel worker's earnings is the board and lodging offered as a part of her wage. When a girl takes a job she does not see her room and has no notion of what the food is like. If she is an experienced worker she does not expect much.

All women cannot make use of the board and lodging offered in a hotel. It depends upon the conditions of their personal life. Married women or **Living-in a disadvantage** women with dependents are **to women with dependents** barred. So, in some hotels, where the same wage is offered to workers living in or out, married women and women with children are forced to accept the cash wage without the board and lodging. Often this worked great hardship to the women whose husbands were out of work. It was difficult, too, for the woman with dependents for whom she had to maintain a home. A number of widows with children were forced to accept the low cash wage. Finding that this wage would not support them, many of them put their children in institutions and lived in. They felt, on the whole, that this was a highly unsatisfactory solution. With night work and a seven-day week, maids could rarely see their children.

The cost of board and room to employees, furnished as it is upon a large scale, is without doubt much less than the cost of the same if purchased retail **Money value placed** by the employee. In order to judge **upon food and lodging** of the value of board and lodging **by the hotels** which is offered by the hotel, it is necessary to have some standards by which to measure it. Hotels have made no attempt to put a money value on lodging and board. The only way an estimate can be made of the cost to hotels is by the difference in wages paid to employees living in and those living out in the same establishment. Even this means is scarcely accurate because, in some cases, the same wage is paid to both and a varying number of meals is eaten by the employees.

A few instances can be given, however. In three hotels where one group of employees have meals and lodging and where the group living out took no meals in the hotel, there was a difference in the wage between the two groups. The difference which may be said to be *the value placed by the hotels on food and lodging* was, in the three hotels, $2.30, $3.04 and $3.46, respectively.

In seven hotels where one group lived in and one group roomed out but ate in, the wage difference illustrates *the value set by the hotel upon lodging*. The difference in wages varied from $1 a week to $2.31 a week.

In the hotels of up-state cities Polish maids are beginning to replace the American workers. One employment manager said, "We like these foreigners. They don't **Living on a** expect to spend so much money, and they'll **hotel wage** put up with more." Again and again the complaint was heard that the hotel wages were insufficient to live on, even when food and lodging were included. Many of the workers found it necessary to buy food in addition to that provided by the hotel in order to keep their health. Those who did not live in the hotels were unable, because of the irregular hour schedules, to take advantage of the cheaper rates of boarding houses for meals. In most cases they had no family connections on which they could depend. They were forced, therefore, to buy their meals at restaurant prices or else to cook them themselves. Workers, whose wage included three meals but no lodging, were not always able to take advantage of the meals offered. So it happened that waitresses and pantry maids, when their day began in the afternoon, often had only one meal in the hotel. Again, if they had family responsibilities, they could often not reach the hotel in time for breakfast. If a maid's day ended early she lost time by staying for supper in the hotel. The result is that many workers eat the noon meal only in the hotel and provide the other meals at their own expense when they are rooming out.

Most of the hotel workers prefer to live out. "You like a room by yourself which you know is clean. These hotel rooms have so many girls in them, and they're all kinds." But those who do live out experience the difficulty of paying rent out of their small wage. One girl, who worked in a New York hotel for $35 a month and meals, had to pay $25 a month for her room. "Of course," she said, "I can't live on that."

A worker in a Rochester hotel, a widow with three children all living at home, earned $10.50 a week with no board or lodging. She said her eldest son was a printer who was out on strike. "He gets $19 a week strike pay," she said, "while I get $10.50 a week for working 7 days. Of course my pay doesn't make me independent. It just helps along. It doesn't go far when you have to buy your own shoes and shoes for a

12-year-old boy." One woman, who received $50 a month and lived out, worked all day in the hotel and then packed candy every evening from 6 to 10 o'clock to make enough money to live on. She had a family to support. Another intelligent American woman, earning $10 a week, was keeping her sick husband in one room for which she paid $8 a month. She had one bed and a table. The rest of the furniture was packing boxes. She had to prepare all the meals in her spare time.

Aside from food and rent, clothing is the largest item in the hotel workers' budget. Both a uniform for work and street clothes are needed. The uniform was furnished by the hotel in only the largest New York City hotels. When charged to the worker it cost about $4.00. She must also furnish, if a chambermaid or waitress, a black waist and skirt for night work. This waist usually costs from $2.00 to $2.50 and the skirt at least $5.00. The waitress needs a number of clean white shirtwaists. Shoes are an important item to both chambermaids and waitresses who are on their feet all their working hours and must be neatly and comfortably shod. Workers complained that they need shoes every three months and that they cost at least $6 a pair.

After the necessary uniforms and a meagre supply of street clothing are paid for, there is little left from the wage for incidentals and to meet emergencies. Doctors and dentists are rarely consulted except in several large hotels where doctors and dentists are employed by the hotel and where workers can have attention at reduced rates. Women workers neglected their teeth through poverty and ignorance. The older bathmaids and maids frequently had only a few snags left. An occulist was an unheard-of expense. Few of the older workers wore glasses even when they had the greatest difficulty in seeing. Some used magnifying glasses to read the newspapers, and others could not read print at all because of the condition of their eyes. Magazines and newspapers were a luxury. Workers never bought them and read only what was given them by guests. Books were never seen. The workers seemed to have neither the energy nor the money for any kind of self-improvement. The younger girls could frequently find someone to take them out for amusement, but for the older workers there was no recreation at all. They complained that they could save nothing for their old age.

How many guests, who pay from $4.50 to $9 a day for their rooms, know that *less than 6¢* of this goes in cash to the chambermaid for her services? In one hotel where these rates are paid, chambermaids receive $300 a year or, allowing for two days off per month and a week's vacation, a little less than 90¢ for a working day. This is for cleaning fifteen rooms. And yet we are told it is for service that we pay so dearly in hotels!

LIVING-IN CONDITIONS

The living-in conditions described in this report are the conditions found by the workers who made the investigation. They lived in ten hotels. These included some of the largest hotels in New York City where a proportion of the women workers always live in.

The food for maids and other women workers is served in "Helps' Hall." When the worker offers to take the new maid "down" to lunch she means it literally. Usually **Food** it is in the second basement underground. Through labyrinths, ill-lighted and heated, sometimes dripping from pipes overhead, she finally arrives at "Helps' Hall." Sometimes she finds it next to a basement laundry which is always steaming hot. As the worker enters, she faces a long row of steam tables. She has her meal ticket punched, grabs a tray, and gets in line. There is no choice of food. Her tray is filled with soup, meat, potatoes and pudding and she deposits it on one of the deal tables in the room and seats herself with the rest on a bench without a back. If she comes late, there is often a litter of spilled food and dirty dishes on the table which take away her appetite. There is a rattle of tin knives and forks. Usually only maids and other women workers are eating in the dining hall, although in small hotels men and women eat at different tables in the same room.

In the hotels in which the workers lived in, they found the dining-room service always hurried. Soup was usually spilled and too much sugar put in the coffee. In one smaller hotel in New York City where men and women ate together workers waited on themselves. All cut their bread from the same loaf, dished out meat at the steam tables, often with the help of their fingers, and poured their own milk. A late worker coming to lunch found messed-over remains of food which had been fingered by many unwashed hands of porters, laundrymen, maids and cleaners.

The quantity of food served was sufficient. Plates were well filled, second helpings were often allowed, tea, coffee, milk, bread and butter were always plentiful. Desserts usually "ran out," but desserts were considered a luxury anyway. The quality of food was inferior. Poor cuts of meat and leftovers in the form of stew and hash with cold bologna for supper was the usual meat diet. Tinned vegetables, carrots, beans and macaroni without cheese were customary. Boiled potatoes were the mainstay. Rice, in different forms, was always served. Rice and bread puddings were the favorite desserts. Butter was often oleomargarine and milk was thin and blue. Fresh vegetables, fresh salads and fruit never appeared even in midsummer. It is true salads and melons were sometimes served, but they were wilted, and workers would not touch them. Ice cream, a very skimmed-milk ice cream, was served once a week on Sundays. Stale French pastries and sour chocolate eclairs sometimes appeared.

The following menus for "Helps' Hall" in a New York hotel illustrate the unvaried, unappetizing and unhealthful food offered. The meals were served on the hottest days of the month of August. Breakfast: Oatmeal, unsalted and with lumps in it, sugar, tea and milk. Lunch: Macaroni without cheese flavored with meat grease, boiled potatoes, bread and corn bread, butter, coffee or tea and unflavored rice pudding. Supper: Fish (which was very strong and unedible), boiled potatoes, bread, butter and tea. Following this supper for lunch the next day there was rice cooked in meat grease with boiled potatoes and stew added. For supper there was stew again, corn bread, coffee, tea and bread pudding flavored with cinnamon.

And so on, every day appeared stew and boiled potatoes during a week of work in this hotel. The workers all complained of the food as not fit to eat. They said, "They don't care what they give you in a hotel. Don't eat most of it, it will kill you. They feed you like dogs here." Many workers did not come to lunch at all. They made a little tea and a sandwich in their rooms. Many others on hot days, after eating such meals, had indigestion and were forced to leave their work. They went out for meals as often as they could, especially for supper. One girl said, "I am so sick of potatoes.

I do want some fresh vegetables and a salad. Of course you can get a real meal sometimes outside, but, Holy God, on our wages!" Another worker was overheard giving advice to a girl who was leaving, "Well, kid, I tell you, it's God's truth this ain't no place for a young American girl like you. When you're young, you can get out. You get into a club, kid, where you get the same grub they eat theirselves. Here, the grub will make you old before your time. Look at me, I'm just thirty and I look fifty. If you stay here, you just get used to the food and everything. You see, they're all old ones here. You get out. Now I just eat a little toast and tea some days. What else do they give you? Potatoes! I tell you to get out, though I hate like hell to see you go."

The food served to pantry workers was much better and they could eat salads and fruit if they cared to. They ate on the job, however, and often had no time to eat their lunches. Waitresses in some hotels ate the same grade of food as maids and kitchen help, but they "picked up" extra food on the side.

The lodging furnished women in large hotels was confined to bed space in a dormitory except in a few instances. The **Lodging** bedrooms varied in size, but were everywhere overcrowded. There were from two to ten girls in a room in most hotels. Cots were placed side by side and the only ventilation came from windows at the far end of the room. The rooms were often overheated and ill-ventilated. Several rooms opened on air shafts. In one hotel there were three occupants in a room with one window opening on a narrow airshaft. The air was "vicious" and it was so dark that an electric light was needed to see at noon.

In one hotel a worker, when shown to her room, was told, "This is an awful nice room, not many people in it." It was a room 10 x 20 feet, with six beds, two dressers, no chairs and a row of lockers. There were two small windows at one end of the room. "There are twice as many girls in the room next door," said the guide. A room in a large metropolitan hotel, 18 feet long, 15 feet wide and 10 feet high, housed eight girls. They slept in double-decker beds. There were two large windows and when the weather was hot enough so everyone was willing to have the windows open, the air was reasonably good. But when it was cold and some one of the eight girls wanted the windows closed, the air in the morning was frightful. Three dressers stood in a curtained space on one side of the room under which the clothes of the eight girls hung together. There was one straight chair apiece. The room was steam-heated, with an electric light hanging from the ceiling. When the girls who slept in the lower berths wanted to read they had to stick their heads out, as the upper berths took away the light. As the girls living in the room worked different shifts, there was always some one asleep, which meant that the rest must keep quiet. A girl coming in at midnight after a night watch had to undress in the dark. One of the maids said, "This room is one of the pleasantest in the house."

In the smaller hotels dormitory rooms were less frequent. In one hotel two girls slept in double decker beds in an 8 x 10 room. In one hotel only were single rooms found, but this hotel had just begun to room its maids and had not yet filled the rooms with two beds apiece.

Beds had adequate linen which was usually clean, though often ragged. Towels and soap were furnished by the hotel in every case. In the larger hotels a maid cared for the rooms and made the beds. In the smaller hotels this was done by the workers, and bedrooms were very carelessly kept. There was an adequate number of baths and toilets in the largest, modern hotels of New York City, although they were often ill-kept and dirty. In the small hotels in New York City and in the hotels of the other cities of the State an inadequate number of baths and toilets were found and the plumbing was poor. Baths were ill-kept and often the hot and cold water faucets were out of order. In some hotels maids were expected to use guests' toilets and showers at odd hours.

Laundry facilities were inadequate except in the largest New York hotels. Maids washed their clothes at night and hung them in their rooms to dry. The damp and unhealthful atmosphere in a bedroom in which wet clothes are hanging can be imagined. In some cases an iron could be secured from the linen room. In others, maids bought their own irons which they attached to electric lights in their rooms. In several hotels maids were required to wash their own uniforms under these conditions and often they washed clothes for the guests.

In no hotel in which the investigators worked was there a room in which women workers could receive guests. For social life they were forced outside the hotel to the streets. In only one hotel was there a telephone in the employees' quarters. Three hotels had rest rooms for women workers with comfortable chairs and tables. Two had victrolas and one had a piano in its rest room. No books or magazines were ever found. In the majority of hotels there was not a comfortable chair which women workers living-in could use while off duty. They spent their recreation hours talking on trunks in the halls or lying on the beds in their rooms.

RECOMMENDATIONS

On the basis of the facts set forth in this report, the Consumers' League of New York believes that there is need for *a special code for the hotel industry*. The nature of the work in hotels is such that regulations regarding the length of hours and the distribution of hours in shifts cannot be made to apply to all occupations alike. Separate arrangements, therefore, must be made for chambermaids, pantry workers, waitresses, etc. The Consumers' League recommends that a more intensive and extensive investigation be made by the State Industrial Commission to secure additional information necessary for drafting such a special code.

A Special Code for the Hotel Industry

The recommendations of the Consumers' League as to points which should be considered in drafting a code for the hotel industry follow.

It is recommended that legislation be passed to make it possible to include in the Industrial Code the regulation of hours of work as well as the actual working conditions and conditions under which women hotel workers live in a hotel.

Hours

Women workers should have 24 hours of consecutive rest in every calendar week.

No woman worker should work more than 8 hours in one day or more than 48 hours in one week.

No woman worker should be allowed to work between the hours of 12 midnight and 6 A. M.

Because it is a continuous industry, workers may be permitted to work broken shifts. Not more than two shifts should be worked in one day. For chambermaids and pantry maids there should be at least four hours between shifts in order that the time may be utilized by the worker. For waitresses there should be two shifts with at least four hours between shifts, or three shifts within a spread of thirteen hours.

Each worker should have a scheduled time for meals. At least one-half hour should be allowed for each meal.

Living-in Conditions

The system of living-in should be abolished.

While the living-in system continues, each worker should have a single room or, if two employees are in one room, there should be single beds, not double deckers. Ventilation should be by window. In the case of airshaft, court of areaway there should be a specified number of feet between the window and the opposite wall. The rooms of workers should be located so that they do not get their air from the laundry or kitchen. Each room should be equipped with a sanitary metal bed, clean and sufficient bedding, a locker, closet or dresser where clothes may be kept sanitary and safe, and at least one comfortable chair.

Sanitary conveniences (toilets, showers and tubs) should be separately enclosed. Those for men and women should be remote from each other and plainly marked. Sanitary conveniences should be clean and light, and there should be a sufficient number to each floor for the number of employees using them.

There should be hospital accommodations provided in accordance with the size of the establishment. The room should have beds so that workers who are ill can be segregated from the other employees.

A sitting room should be provided, quiet, with comfortable chairs, where visitors are permitted.

The food served to workers should constitute a well-balanced diet, wholesome, varied, appetizing and sufficient in quantity. It should be served in a well-lighted and aired, quiet and clean dining room.

A Minimum Wage Law

The Consumers' League recommends that a minimum wage law be passed in New York State which shall include the hotels in its application.

Tipping

Tipping should be abolished.

SUGGESTIONS TO HOTEL MANAGERS

It is suggested that it be the duty of special employees to care for the workers' rooms and also to serve the meals, remove the dishes and keep the tables clean in the employees' dining room or cafeteria.

It is suggested that employees be interviewed and hired by a person understanding the technique of the selection of workers and the requirements of the various jobs in the hotel, with the purpose of securing an efficient force of workers and reducing the turnover of labor. An experienced person, preferably a woman, should be responsible for the introduction of the new employee to her job, her training, her transfer or promotion.

The conditions of living-in, while the system is continued, should be under the supervision of a competent woman.

Behind the Scenes

in

Canneries

֍

Investigation Conducted by

THE CONSUMERS' LEAGUE OF NEW YORK

1930

Behind the Scenes

in

Canneries

Published — *April, 1930*

The Consumers' League of New York
150 Fifth Avenue
New York City

This investigation was planned and made by Miss Marjorie White. She was assisted in the field work by Miss Edith Dudley. The Consumers' League Committee, under whom the study was made, put into final shape the reports of the investigators. The members of the Committee take this opportunity to express their appreciation of the work done by the investigators, particularly in view of the hardships to which they were subjected during their employment in the canneries.

FOREWORD

IT is welcome news, as this report is ready for publication, to learn that the New York State Canners' Association at its annual meeting agreed to co-operate with the State Department of Labor in giving attention day by day to the problems of overtime in order to work out some scientific solution of this vexing question, and to ask its members to abide strictly by the provisions of the child labor and safety laws.

The Consumers' League planned its inquiry and collected the facts contained in this report before the canners had been aroused to take action by the stirring words of the Industrial Commissioner. Our report shows an archaic disregard in many canneries for the workers' health and comfort and little up-to-date conception of the gain in production, quantity and quality, that follows changes such as we suggest. With the shortness of the season, June through October, as an excuse, the canners have continued working in old, inadequate quarters without many essential improvements. With the perishability of the raw material as an excuse, they have said they must work overtime when the ripe fruit and vegetables come in from the farms and have been permitted exceptions from the labor laws to do so. Although other industries are held to the 51-hour law, they are allowed to employ women up to 66 hours a week at the peak of the season. Yet, after all, these are only the ordinary problems of management and the workers should not be called on to carry the burden due to lack of planning for these ever recurring emergencies. Wages are, we believe, among the lowest paid in the state—usually $10.20 or $12.75 for a 51-hour week. From necessity, the women work overtime as long as strength holds out, whatever the sacrifice in health.

These are the basic facts that must be faced at what we hope is the parting of the ways—between the old and the new. It is toward solving these problems, emulating the new practices of their industry in other states, that the co-operation of the canners and the Industrial Commissioner will be directed. There can be no doubt that the hoped for changes will, if sufficiently comprehensive, be of lasting benefit, not only to employers but to workers in the whole industry. Public support should be given their efforts, and our report will acquaint the public with present conditions and furnish standards that must be taken into consideration when the adequacy of the proposed changes are judged.

MARY W. DEWSON,
President of the Consumers' League of New York.

INTRODUCTION

For many years the canning industry of New York has been of interest to the public because of the large number of women employed, and also, unfortunately, because of its undesirable conditions of work. Successive investigations—an important one by the Factory Investigating Commission in 1913—have shown the evils of long hours of work for women, and the existence of widespread child labor. The present investigation was undertaken on account of the lively interest of the consumer in food industries; and especially because it was strongly indicated that conditions of work were not satisfactory.

New York State is maintaining an important position in the canning industry. It is the second most important state in the country in the number of persons engaged in the industry, only California outnumbering it. It is the third most important both in the value of the product, and in number of canneries. Only California and Maryland exceed it in number of plants. It continues to lead all other states in the output of green and wax beans, in sauerkraut, and in apple sauce.

The Consumers' League decided to make an investigation by sending workers into the canneries because it believed that in this manner the truest picture could be obtained. Owing to the prolonged drought of last summer, the cannery season was late and short, but our investigators were active in the field from the beginning of July to the end of September, the peak months of the canning period. They worked in both large and small plants well distributed through the cannery zone. Besides obtaining information from other workers, they themselves experienced as employees the conditions in plants employing about 10% of all the women in the industry. We are of the opinion, therefore, that their reports represent an accurate cross-section of the conditions existing in the summer of 1929. The facts ascertained are fully corroborated by those of previous cannery studies.

General Findings

Decrease of Child Labor.   One of the encouraging facts that has come to our attention is the decrease in the number of children employed.   As contrasted with the findings of 1913, there has been a definite reduction in the number of children employed for the hand snipping of beans.   This is to some extent due to the introduction of snipping machinery, but it is also evident that the canners themselves have taken steps to keep the children out of the sheds.

Less Lifting.   The use of machinery for bean snipping has also lessened the amount of heavy work and lifting that formerly was a hardship for the women.

Illegal Overtime.   On the other hand, in New York, women are still employed for excessively long hours, and often at night, in both cases in violation of the state labor law.

Low Wage Rates.   Twenty or 25 cents an hour, that is, $10.20 or $12.75 a week for the usual factory week of 51 hours, is so little that the workers welcome overtime regardless of their health.

Antiquated Employment Methods.   The canners do not use business-like methods to secure all possible local help.   The practice of exceeding the daily capacity of their plants and relying upon overtime employment instead of securing more help, seems as marked in those otherwise progressive canneries as in the ones less well equipped.

Undue Exposure.

1.   The shed workers, as a rule, are not protected from inclement weather, but are often exposed to rain and cold, which results in illness and consequent irregularity of attendance.

2.   Many women work on wet floors all day, and in some occupations they are wet to the skin because of dripping

belts and tables. Since the weather is often cold, such wetness may be a menace to health.

Unnecessary Noise. The noise of machinery other than that at which women are employed, but close to them, is a constant source of discomfort and so distracts their attention as to impair efficiency.

Concerning these important matters, there is little evidence of change which might well be expected of forward-looking management after the Factory Investigating Commission's report in 1913. This is especially disappointing in view of the progress made by competing plants in Wisconsin and California. The latter two, by developing extensive systems of adjusting raw materials to plant capacity, by organizing the labor supply, and by setting minimum wage rates including higher rates for overtime beyond the basic day, have made it possible for hours of work to be regulated, and have made it a matter of pride to provide working conditions of far greater comfort and efficiency.

We have given special attention to the environment of the worker presenting the findings as to such concrete conditions as wetness, exposure to weather, noise of machines, etc. The important sections on hours and wages are given last. In order to show graphically the conditions found, we shall quote liberally from the reports of our investigators. We believe that these throw new light on some of the chief defects of management that are now a reflection on the industry. They also show some of the improvements that progressive canners have adopted.

WHAT THE WORK IS LIKE

The investigators were employed at practically all of the usual cannery processes which women do. In order to make clear the picture of the work, a brief statement of the processes is given here.

Peas. The first rush of cannery work comes in the pea season. Peas are run on moving belts past the workers who pick out by hand the shucks, hard peas, and occasional pebbles and thistle buds. All the other processes for peas, such as the filling, capping of cans, and cooking, are done by machinery which is tended by men.

Beans. The bean season follows and lasts longer than any other. Hand snipping is still done, but machines are used for snipping beans increasingly. They were found in four-fifths of the canneries visited. The snipped beans, like the peas, pass over the sorting belts so that any defective ones or those that are too small or too large can be picked out by the women, who also push the beans into cans and weigh them.

Corn. Corn comes unhusked to the cannery shed and is brought to the worker either through chutes from an upper story, or by men who lift it from the floor and put it into position for the women to feed into the machines. The husk is torn off by metal fingers and as the ear falls, the nub is cut off by a knife in the machine. The ears go on to the sorting belt where the women pull or cut off any part of the husk that is not removed by the machines, and any spoiled or discolored kernels.

Tomatoes. Tomatoes are scalded before they reach the tables where the women peel them by hand, remove the stem, and cut out any bad spots. This work is one of the wettest operations for women.

Little skill is needed for any of the hand operations of preparing fruits and vegetables for canning. The one important machine at which women were found at work is the corn huskers. Owing to the use of sanitary cans, women are no longer required for the minute inspection which was formerly needed before the final sealing of the old type can.

THE MOVING BELT

Most of the women find work at the sorting tables difficult because the constant watching of moving objects strains their eyes. Many declare that it makes them feel dizzy and sick. They try to overcome this feeling by looking up the belt, or fixing their eyes on a still object at frequent intervals, by leaving the belt for a few moments, or by standing frequently. Some of the women say they are troubled most during the last hours of a five-hour stretch, when they are tired and hungry, or when the belt is speeded up too much.

The investigators found that complaints increased when the belts were shaking and jolting due to the vibration of the attached machine (snipper), or to some defect or improper adjustment. And of course the discomfort was greatest when the corn, peas, or beans "danced a jig" as they passed along. Sometimes this jiggling occurred spasmodically, and sometimes for several hours continuously.

Our workers reported that their eyes were very tired after a day's work at the belt, and frequently their fellow workers said they had a headache at the end of the day.

The following illustrations are taken from the investigators' notes.

Edna G. told me after lunch today that she had a splitting headache. "Working at the sorting table always makes me seasick," she said. Others complained of tired eyes and nausea. Mrs. R. said she tried to read her newspaper at lunch and the letters kept bobbing up and down just like the beans on the belt.

The bean sorting table shook most of the day. Before lunch and about 4 o'clock I suddenly felt dizzy and blinked my eyes and closed them hard, then fixed them on a stack of pea vines standing outside. "Getting sea-sick?" asked Mrs. B. who had been watching me. I nodded my head. "I guess you're needing food," she said. "I used to get sea sick. When I get kinda empty inside, I go to the washroom or stand outdoors." The foreman came to our table to inspect the beans. I told him I was dizzy. "These tables need new underpinnin's," he said. "I tighten 'em up and they stop shaking for awhile but work loose again in no time. I say the snippers are run too fast. The whole thing's adjusted for a set speed. Running it faster knocks it loose."

We had "chops" all the morning. (Chops are beans of all sizes and shapes which will be cut in small pieces before they are canned.) The beans "danced a jig" as they passed me, for the moving belt vibrated as though it had pebbles underneath. This jiggling occurred spasmodically for half-hour periods in the morning and was continuous most of the afternoon. After lunch I told Earle, the machinist, the shaking of the belt hurt my eyes. "It's the machines," he said, "they're built wrong. We've worked over 'em, but we can't stop it!"

Mrs. Rogers said, "It was worse in peas. My eyes used to hurt and water at night when I went to bed. I don't get dizzy like some of the women do, but I get a headache in beans once in a while. Mrs. K. can't work at sorting more'n an hour. This belt don't jump about so much as the other one. It's a newer one."

Quality of Product Injured by Speeding of the Machine

The canner asserts that perfect grading according to size is one of the first requisites of the market. What amazed the investigators was that the standards of work set up were so completely disregarded through the speeding of the machines, the lack of supervision, or any regard for the worker's capacity to maintain the same standard after a time.

The words of Joe B., who said he had worked in canneries for 8 years, expressed the viewpoint of others in regard to the quality of the work, when he said, "I can't make 'em out. They (company) orders one kind of sortin', and expects the women to keep at it for ten, twelve, maybe fourteen hours. The stuff that goes into them cans ain't much like the order!"

No matter how many hours Mrs. I. worked, the speed of the belt was such that she thought it was necessary for her to push back the beans that she did not have time to sort properly. The workers considered her an intelligent, conscientious worker. One day she remarked, "The number of 'iron' beans they let go over the belt is fierce. And, my dear, nobody seems to care. Now don't mind what I do. I tell you, let 'em go by, and don't kill yourself."

All day long yellow beans poured on to the belt. The women sorted out as many imperfect beans as they could, as the conveyor carried them past, but could not begin to sort them all. Two women frantically pushed them back with their hands in hope that the stream would soon slacken up. But the snippers poured out the beans so rapidly that the belt brought them the piles they had pushed back. The foreman came to the belt. "It's no good to push 'em back," he said. "You'll never catch up that way. Get all you can and let the rest go." The women relaxed, sorted as fast as they could. The investigator wondered what happened to all of the unsorted beans.

John regulated the speed at which he poured the peas on to the belt. The speed seldom bore any relation to the quantity of peas to be cleaned. "If the belt is too fast, pick out those you can, and let the rest go by," he said.

At the end of a half an hour, I realized that the speed of the bean belt was such that Mrs. G. and I could not attempt to accomplish what we had been directed to do: clean out all the leaves, stems, dirt and sticks, and snip off the beans the snipper had failed to snip. I slowed down my pace. Mrs. G. asked me if I was tired—tired at eight in the morning. "I will be soon if I work so fast," I told her. Then I observed that the other seven girls at our table did but one part of the sorting they had been ordered to do.

The speed at which the cherries came on to the belt was regulated almost entirely by Sam. Usually he poured so fast that we could not pick out all the defective cherries. Occasionally the foreman pushed back the cherries on to the belt or asked Sam to pour more slowly. Many defective cherries went into the conveyor.

At the pea belt there were periods of work at high speed when the peas were poured on to the belt so fast and were consequently so thick that it was impossible to get all the thistles, shucks and hard peas as they passed. These periods alternated with waits of 3 to 13 minutes when there were no peas ready for John to pour on to the belt.

All these stories emphasize not only the disregard of the workers' comfort, but also the lack of proper supervision to insure carrying out right standards of workmanship.

WORKERS EXPOSED TO EXTREME COLD AND HEAT

Canneries are usually great barrack-like buildings built of wood, without heating equipment in which the workers are exposed to chilling draughts in the cold weather that often prevails in the months when the canneries are working. Even in the summer months the early morning and night hours are often very chilly and at the end of the season, which lasts into October, frosts are not infrequent. Also, the constant opening of doors allows cold winds to sweep through the work rooms. On the other hand, when the machines are running, these same rooms may be full of steam and so hot as to be unbearable. Two pictures of different canneries from the investigators' reports are given here.

For the past three mornings in August, from 4 until 7 a. m.—when the sun rises—the process building is so cold I cannot stop shivering, and my stiff fingers snip the beans awkwardly and slowly. The 40 or 50 women working at tables wear heavy woolen sweaters over old coats and sit huddled up to keep from getting colder. A few have scarfs around their necks. Some of them have put their feet in empty wooden boxes. "Don't they ever heat the building?" I ask Marie, who sits beside me in a man's heavy overcoat. "Not since I been here . . . They call this summer work, that's why . . . You got to freeze 'til they start the machines. They'll heat us up by noon."

The wind has blown a gale all day, but the temperature indoors is rising. All doors are closed and all windows except one in which the bottom half of glass has been broken out. The smell of beans and steam becomes nauseating, but is preferable to the blast of cold air which enters whenever the door behind our backs is opened by the men going to and from the open shed. "When that door is closed I sweat and when it's open I get chilled. If I don't have a cold tomorrow, I'll know it," are the words of Mrs. J. At noon Mrs. R asks the assistant superintendent to move the tables so that we may face the door when it opens and shuts. "No time today," is his brisk answer. By 4 o'clock the women complain of heavy heads, of damp bodies, aches, and chapped hands. "I wanted to go to a dance tonight," Edna D. tells us regretfully. "But I feel more like going to bed after a day like this. I've got a sore throat." "Days like this, my rheumatism gets me," Mrs. K. replies.

When work is done in cannery sheds, which are of light frame construction open on two or three sides, exposure to the weather is even more serious. Beans must be snipped and corn husked regardless of the weather. Experiences from the investigators' reports are quoted.

It got steadily colder all the morning. At 11 o'clock there was a flurry of snow. Everybody shivered. My heavy coat kept out some of the cold. I put my hat on as the other women did. A sharp wind swept through the shed on both sides and blew under the tables over our legs. We put our feet inside boxes to get them off the damp, concrete floor. This made them a little warmer but was not as good as a gunny sack. Most of the women were warmly dressed, wearing heavy old coats. The little old lady at the next belt told me she put on a woolen dress and woolen stockings today for she caught cold yesterday. We joked with the foreman, asking for steam pipes or a stove under the table. He laughingly replied he had ordered them. The wind increased. My feet were numb with cold. I stamped them noisily up and down in my box. The shivering women rubbed their hands and all the talk was of the cold.

At noon, half frozen, the women hurried for sunny spots and food. Mrs. K. and I went upstairs to the can loft where sunshine flooded the dirty, cluttered room. After eating our lunch, we went downstairs to the cooking room where many of us lingered to share the welcome warmth of the steam from the open "retorts." At one o'clock, everyone went back to the sunless, windy snipping shed. By three o'clock it was a little warmer. The woman opposite me looked ill. When she coughed, she said it hurt way down in her chest and ached in her shoulders. The lame woman next me said, "I just dread tomorrow." "You'd better not come," I advised her. "I sorta feel as though I oughta," she said. At six o'clock the day was over. We hurried home.

At another cannery the story is the same.

Everyone at the bean filling tables in the process room complained of the chill and dampness. At 10:30 a. m. the superintendent came inside and said, "You women get busy outside in the shed at the corn." After he had gone the women, already chilled and cold, got together and decided that since a bitter wind was sweeping through the open shed they would not go outside until canvas curtains were stretched on both sides of the sorting belt. Mrs. K., an overworked little woman, explained, "I asked the superintendent to put them up yesterday. Mrs. B. asked him twice. They don't stop the cold but they keep the wind from blowing in on us. They was up last year. He's got them in the store house."

The superintendent appeared again and ordered the women outside at once. Mrs. B. asked him to put up the canvas, while the women began putting on their extra wraps. He made no definite answer. In the open shed the wind cut through the women's clothing. Although wearing two pairs of stockings, long underwear, two sets of undervests, slips, wash dress, a lined winter coat, and two woolen sweaters, I shivered. Each of us wore rubbers, or galoshes, and stuck our feet and legs into a gunny sack and a box, and then placed boxes around our feet to break the force of the wind. After sorting cold wet ears of corn for half an hour the hands of the women were red and stiff, their eyes were watering from the cold, and the positions in which they sat showed they were shivering and wretched. All conversation was of the cold and the attitude of the management. The women said that they could not endure another half hour and talked of quitting.

At 11 o'clock when, owing to the bunching of corn the power was turned off, the women rushed into the open yard beside the shed, stamping their feet, and trying to get warm. Mrs. B. led the group. "Will you strike?" she asked each woman. The answers were "yes" and while waiting for the superintendent the women raced about, waving arms, and stamping feet. At 11:10 the power was turned on and the corn started moving over the belt. But the women agreed they would not go back until the canvas was put up. Ten minutes went by. Then the superintendent came from the shed. "If you will go back at once those canvas curtains will be put up in an hour," he said. By noon the canvas was up. The force of the wind was broken, but the cold grew steadily worse. The women sat sorting cold corn with half frozen fingers all afternoon, and until 9:30 that night.

IT IS HARD TO KEEP DRY IN A CANNERY

Water is used in almost all the canning processes; for washing of corn and cherries, for the blanching of peas, beans and beets, and for the scalding of tomatoes. Consequently, water and steam keep the machines wet while in operation, and all too frequently the floors as well.

There were drains in the floors of all canneries to carry off the water, but in a number of cases the drain failed to serve the purpose effectively and the water ran to other parts of the floor. When the sorting and filling tables were near the machines the women working at them had their feet constantly wet, sometimes for hours at a stretch. Even when there were drains to carry off the water from the machines, the leakiness of many of the tables prevented the women workers from keeping dry.

Wooden slats, which should be provided according to the industrial code governing canneries, were found in only about half of the positions where they should have been. Most of them were too low and did not keep the feet of the workers above the water. Some women wore rubbers. The following comments are indicative.

> Water from the blanching machine ran down under one of the bean sorting tables. The women sat with their feet upon boxes in order to keep dry. To get from the husking machine to any other part of the building, and not get their feet wet, the women have to walk with their heels. Some wear rubbers, others object to the warmth of an overshoe. Water leaks from the washing machine, the conveyors and sorting belts. Several times a day a man sweeps away the water, but it immediately collects under foot.

Occasionally the management provided the women with rubber aprons which were some protection when they were peeling and filling tomatoes and trimming beets. In most places the women had to provide their own aprons and rubbers for work on corn, cherries, and beans. They complained that the management made them meet this expense.

"They used to give us knives and rubber aprons here," said a girl. "Now you have to get your own." "Sure they don't give you nothing these days," replied the woman opposite me.

One of the investigators tells of her own experiences.

About 9:30 I felt my underclothing above the knee was wet. Try as I did to keep my dress and sweater from touching the wet, slippery wooden tables and trays, my clothing was soaked to the skin. I left the table until I found a gunny sack which I tied about my hips with a piece of rope. By 10 o'clock the gunny sack was wet. Searching for another, I found a piece of heavy, dirty canvas. I tied it about my waist and found it covered me from neck to knees. "It's better than nothing," I said when the women working at my table laughed at my appearance. "If you want to keep dry here you got to get your aprons and rubbers. They give you a knife for corn sorting, but nothing else."

TOO MANY STANDING OCCUPATIONS AND 'MOST OF SEATING POOR

There is a great deal of unnecessary standing at the cannery jobs and, even when chairs are provided, the women cannot sit comfortably at their work on account of the faulty construction of the sorting tables or other equipment.

When filling the cans or feeding the corn husking machines, the women usually stand; often for the whole day without having seats provided. It was only in a few places that women stood at the sorting tables. Every conceivable kind of seating arrangement is found varying from a good type of adjustable steel chair or a wooden chair with a back, to a motley assortment of stools, crates or boxes. This will be seen from descriptions of seating at different canneries.

> Over 100 women sat at wooden tables snipping beans by hand. They sat on all kinds of seats, steel stools, wooden chairs with wire backs, and piled up boxes. There was no question among them as to which they preferred. Whenever a woman having a chair with a back left it for more than a moment, it disappeared and was replaced with a stool, or nothing at all. "You don't get tired so fast if your back can rest while you're working," was the reason given to us by Mrs. R. when we joked about this habit among the workers.

> The girl opposite me pointed to her round shoulders and her body humped over the table. I saw that the height of the stool she was sitting on compelled her to sit sideways, her legs stretched straight to the floor. This posture was taken by many of the women. Others sat with their elbows below the level of the table and so had to reach up for handfuls of beans.

Many of the women were sitting at their jobs in very uncomfortable positions.

After I had stood an hour at the bean sorting belt, the woman at the next belt brought my partner an iron stool and an empty box for a foot rest. She pointed to a pile of empty boxes saying, "You can pile up boxes for a seat." I put one box on another close to the belt and sat down. My feet were on the floor, my knees under the table, but I sat too high at the belt to let my arms work comfortably. My partner sat sideways on her stool with her feet on the box. "Why do you sit sideways?" I asked, thinking how tired the muscles of her side and back must get in that position. She motioned under the table. The frame inclosing the moving belt underneath made it impossible for anyone to sit in the proper position and put her knees under the table.

My shoulders soon tired and I stood up to work. C., a young Italian girl, stood beside me for a few moments, then got a box, sitting sideways on it without a footstool. From where I worked I could see, at the other end of the shed, a moving belt rise to the grader at an angle of about 60 degrees. Here Italian women sat sideways on boxes, stools and chairs, because a frame around the belt prevented their knees from getting under the table. Near by two inclined sorting belts extended from the top of the cutting machine (about 7 feet high) to within 18 inches of the floor. The girls working on either side of it sat on low wooden boxes. At the belt of one of the filling machines a girl was kneeling on a wooden box. As each filled can of beans passed her she pressed them down with a blunt wooden pestle, one stroke for each can. Later in the day I asked her how she liked the work. "I get awful tired in no time," was her answer.

When the forewoman placed me at the sorting belt, there was no seat. But the height at which the belt moved past was too low to work comfortably standing. Finally someone gave me a wooden chair made of slats. I tried it, but the back tilted outward and gave no support. There were a few of these chairs at the belts, but most of the women used boxes. The girls opposite me complained of tired backs. They rested their elbows on the edge of the table as they worked. The work was done in such a slovenly fashion that beans, dark, wilted, and broken went by on their way to the cutting machine.

At the corn sorting belt in the other end of the shed, the women sat sideways on low chairs or boxes and put their feet on boxes. The belt was low and a board along the side kept their knees from getting under it. No one could stand up and work because the belt was on a level slightly above the knees. After three hours each day of this work, I was so tired that I had to make myself "stick out" the hours with the other women. After four hours I tried not to change the position of my body as any motion caused muscle aches in my back and shoulders. The foreman of the cutting machines inside the process house came to the belt two different nights, and complained of the women's work. For a half hour following these moments they grabbed at the corn and sent him clean ears. Then they did not care about complaints. They slumped back into their tired positions and continued a bad quality of work, half sick with cold and fatigue.

In another place, the women sat sideways on wire backed chairs which were raised on small boxes. The seats were hard, so a gunny sack or sweater was added. Frequently, when a woman changed her position, she complained that she could not sit facing her work and put her knees under the belt. The position quickly cramped her muscles. Turning the other side to the belt was the only change one could make. "When I can't sit no more, I go to the washroom and jump up and down," was the complaint of one young girl.

The sitting position of two women at a belt, on to which

beans from the five sorting tables fall, was very bad. The belt was about 12 inches from the floor. Cramped into a narrow space, they sat on low boxes picking out the bad beans that the women on the sorting tables failed to catch. "That belt could have been higher," a woman said one day when the two women complained of extreme crampedness and backache. "They get 5 cents more an hour for working there, though. But Mr. S. has to beg women to work there. It's an awful position. I did it once, and I won't no more." After four o'clock each day the girl sitting beside me took her chair off the wooden box and sat so her knees got under the belt. I copied her motions and found the tiredness in my back and knees was lessened somewhat, but the strain in my shoulders increased. An ache in the back of my neck developed and stayed there for several days.

The investigators reported so many instances where they, together with the other workers, had been standing all day at their work or sitting in cramped positions, that it is impossible to quote them all. Only a few more instances can be given. The following refer especially to standing.

Packing of beans at the two filling tables could only be done standing. The women at the first "line" stood 10½ hours one day, from 7:30 a. m. to 12, and from 12:45 to 7 p. m. The only rest periods were those they took in the washroom, where they could sit down. Once when a delay occurred on the "line" on which I worked, I tried sitting on two different kinds of stools used at the snipping table. I was so tired that I remarked to Mrs. Reese I could lie down on one of the empty bean tables and fall asleep. "Don't you suppose we all get that way?" said Mrs. Reese, who was so tired that her hands fumbled with the beans she was pushing into a can. The Polish woman, who lived in the cannery camp, rubbed her back and sighed. "Every night I'm tired the same as tonight. I get a pain in my side when I stand so long." The skill with which the women filled the cans decreased as the day grew older; so did the number of cans.

Sixteen women stood at the packing tables pushing beans into cans. "I've worked here the last five years and nobody's ever sat at these tables," said Mrs. P. "Nobody could sit at them; they must be 40 years old. This place needs some new filling tables." The tables were wooden, old and very heavy. If the obstructions underneath were removed and the seats the right height it would be possible for a worker to sit.

In the open shed, where it had been cold the past week, the women never sat while operating three of the ten husking machines. When the "line" stopped they would rest on piles of unhusked corn spread over the shed floor. "Standing is hard on my feet but I can work better."

"I got so tired sitting, my shoulders ache so. I ain't the right height for this belt," was the remark of one worker. It was impossible to sit at the filling tables. They were not built so that sitting was possible and the space beside the conveyor was too small to hold a seat of any kind.

The women employed at the corn husking machines in one cannery visited, were supplied with chairs. They could either stand or sit, but the structure of the machines interfered so much with the use of the chairs that they usually found it easier to stand.

Each woman, feeding a corn husking machine, was provided with a steel chair having a back. From a shelf before which she sat or stood, the worker fed the ears into the machine which was at one side. After two hours of work, the women stood longer than they sat. Two reasons for this were experienced by the investigator. It was easier to shut off and turn on the power when standing. Sometimes when the ears of corn jammed the mouth of the chute, the worker had to stand and pull them down on to the shelf. After three hours of this stretching and pulling, shoulders and back ached. After five hours, some of the women stood up only when clogging of the machine made it necessary, for even the short irregular periods of sitting somewhat relieved the pain in the back. During the afternoon the women called the foreman frequently to start the machines, and to pull down the ears of corn from the jammed chute.

When I got tired, I resented a 4-inch board nailed against the edge of the shelf to keep the corn from dropping on to my lap or on to the floor. It served this purpose, but in reaching the ears I had to lift my arms above the wooden board or rub them along on it. After several hours, my arms, wrists and shoulders ached and the skin on my forearms became sensitive and red. At noon time the women showed each other this irritation of their forearms. One afternoon, P., in answer to this complaint, sawed off the top half of two of these obstructions. The women said it helped.

Only one plant seemed to recognize the importance of having women seated in comfortable positions. They provided a chair with a modelled wooden seat which was very comfortable. The feet rested easily on the floor and the curved back gave support. However, the working posture had not been studied with sufficient care and provision made for different occupations as the following shows.

The chair was just too low for the height of the belt as the cardboards and cushions many workers used on the seats proved conclusively. Had it been adjustable, this difficulty would have disappeared. Most of the women sat at the belt with shoulders slightly raised, forearms resting on the edge of the belt for support. One girl at the belt complained of backache. She stood up occasionally for relief showing that had the belt been designed for both standing and sitting with equal comfort, fatigue would have been greatly decreased.

All the women stood while peeling tomatoes at this cannery. Occasionally, when anyone got tired she took one of the metal stools standing about the shed. The tables at which they worked were too high to sit comfortably. The deep pan holding the hot tomatoes necessitated working far enough above the pan in order to give freedom of motion to the arms. The girls who filled the cans or glass jars with tomatoes stood on a wooden slatted platform placed a few inches from the floor. They filled the jars or cans on a tray in front of them by scooping up the tomatoes with their hands from the moving belt. Sitting for this job would have been almost impossible because of the wide wooden frame on either side of the table enclosing the moving belt. To raise her arms to a good working position on a sorting belt, one woman put several layers of thick cardboard on the seats of her stool or chair or laid a wooden tray across it. I found neither comfortable. When I put my sweater under me I saw that other women had put a coat or gunny sack on top of the seat. A few women slumped at their work, leaning their arms on the edge of the belt.

UNNECESSARY NOISE HANDICAP TO WORKERS

The effect of noise on men and women is more and more being recognized as injurious to both their health and efficiency. It is, of course, not always possible to provide a quiet work place but if the noise in a factory can be lessened, every effort should certainly be made to bring this about. Yet the story that comes from the canneries shows a surprising lack of understanding of this factor. The amount of noise to which the women are subjected, as shown in the following sketches, makes it clear why they complained about it so much.

After working in a room where five snipping machines and the cutters and the motors that run them are in operation, one woman said, "The noise gets me some days. I'm sure I'd not be so tired if there weren't no noise." Another woman said, "Sometimes the noise makes your head throb and your ears ring."

Today the blanching and grading machines, while at a distance from the snipping machines, rattled and clattered at times so loudly that the women would scowl aand look in their direction. "They have noiseless typewriters, wonder when they'll have noiseless machinery," one woman remarked when the noise seemed particularly irritating. Mrs. A. complained of headache this afternoon. "It's the noise, I guess. It gets in my ears. It's just like the machines was on top of us—that blancher clatters like it was tearin' itself in two.

"Why must the machines make so much noise ?" I asked the foreman at noon today. "They're old and need repairs."

"I get so tired at night I sit ten minutes and go to bed. It's the noise, and watchin' that bean belt that knocks me out. Every year it's the same, girls don't stay long here."

Lack of consideration for the comfort of the workers while cleaning factory equipment is another source of noise. Thus snipping machines were cleaned by forcing live steam from a hose into the hundreds of tiny perforations of the revolving cylinders where the beans get stuck. The noise is terrific while the cleaning lasts. According to one machinist, the "snippers" are supposed to be cleaned at night after work, and sometimes during lunch time. But several canneries cleaned them while the women worked at the sorting tables—which are attached to one end of the machine—one firm repeating this operation four times in a ten-hour day. The stories of the investigators show the great discomfort and stoppage of work caused by this practice.

After two hours of sorting beans my ears were suddenly shocked by a terrific blast of live steam but ten feet away, as it rushed forth against the revolving cylinder of the machines. I clapped my hands to my ears as did most of the women at the five tables. There were five snippers to be cleaned and the noise continued for nine or ten minutes. When it was over I was slightly deafened in both ears. This happened several times daily while I was employed. Thereafter when the steam opened up I left the belt aand waited in the washroom until it was over. The remarks of some of the women were pointed: "They ought to shut off the machines." "They ought to tell the women to go away. It only takes a few minutes; but it makes you deaf for hours." "I get the ear ache if I stay at the belt." "They should have another way of doing it." "I get so deaf I can't work good."

At 4:30 o'clock, one "grader" was shut down. The machinist began to clean it with a hose of live steam as I had seen the "snippers" cleaned during the lunch hour. The grader was about fifteen feet away from me on my left side. As the steam rushed forth with a terrific blast, every woman at the belt looked up and continued to watch the process as I did. "Hey you," the foreman shouted at us, and the women bent their heads to their snipping while the steam roared in our ears. At the first blast I had covered my left ear with my hand, and my face showed irritation. I saw C. look at me, then quickly at the foreman to see whether he had noticed how disturbed I was. The foreman stood over us while the steam roared around the grader for about five minutes. A second grader further away was hosed for another four or five minutes. Everyone was apprehensive and restive.

UNSYSTEMATIZED HOURS

In the peak season, especially of peas, June 15th to August 5th, there is the greatest demand for labor and the New York State Labor Law allows women over 18 years to be employed a 12-hour day and a 66-hour week in the canneries. For the rest of the year, however, the 10-hour day and 60-hour week prevail. At no time does the law allow a woman to be employed before six in the morning or after ten o'clock at night.

Because of the dry summer and the lateness of the pea crop, our investigators could not get much work during the peak season. But after August 5th, in the canneries in which they were employed, their hours were often in violation of the law.

Work for Longer than a Ten-Hour Day

To illustrate, on the first day in one cannery an investigator had her time card punched in at 8 a. m. and out a few minutes after midnight, with an hour for lunch and for dinner, showing a working day of 14 hours and 6 minutes. The second day her card read 8 a. m. to 8:30 p. m. and the third day 7:30 a. m. to 9 p. m. which, omitting the time for meals, made up a total of 11½ hours each day. Such overtime was, of course, illegal.

Why long hours make it impossible for the workers to maintain a high standard the following shows.

For the first half hour after supper, from 7 to 7:30, the women tried to let only the best grade of corn pass by on the sorting belt. They threw out all of the bad and dried ears, cut off the husks not removed by the machines, and cut out the black spots. The fatigue they had known from three until six in the afternoon returned; and the increasing cold that came with the darkness attacked their enthusiasm and they cared less and less what bad corn went by with the good. Even the bucket of hot coffee which Mrs. K.'s husband distributed to them in tin cans at 9 p. m. and the sandwiches or cakes some women had brought, failed to decrease to any great extent their fatigue and make possible better attention.

At 11 o'clock I felt as though I could not possibly endure another hour of the cold and enveloping fatigue. I shifted my attention frequently trying not to fall asleep. I stared at the pump beyond in the open yard; I watched a tall tree swaying to one side in the driving wind. I stood up and sat down. I kept telling myself I must not fall on to the belt, as I had seen another woman do. I watched the other women trying, as desperately as I, to keep awake. Finally Mrs. K. nodded twice and slumped forward toward the moving belt. As she fell Mrs. G. yelled at her and threw a wet ear of corn at her shoulder. The shock of the corn hitting her jerked her back from the belt. She stood up and left the belt saying, "To keep awake I've got to walk." I left the belt, too, and went with her to the washroom. There we stayed as long as we dared, but there was still another hour or more of work.

Work During the Night

At another cannery where an investigator worked all night from 7 p. m. to 5 a. m., the superintendent upon learning that she lived in a nearby town said, "Come at 7 tonight, and if you see any of those girls from C. . . . bring them along." The hours from 10 p. m. to 5 a. m. were, of course, illegal. Instead of using the time clock, the superintendent kept the names of the women in a small book against which he checked their hours. The following sketch will show how much the work deteriorated in quality during the night.

Last night, at 11 p. m., after four hours of work, I suddenly felt dizzy. When I felt better, I told the woman next to me about it. "Guess you haven't seen the half kid," she replied. "Wait until 3 o'clock in the morning. See that fat woman over there? She fainted the first night she was here. They had to carry her out. She's almost asleep." I watched the woman's fat hands move aimlessly over the beans without picking up any. Her mouth and red-lidded, staring eyes showed how fatigued she was. At midnight after we had eaten our lunch, the talk was all about how hard it is to get enough sleep in the day time when one has to work at night. Four Italian women stretched themselves out on the wooden floor to rest. Another laid down on the one cot in the washroom.

At 2 a. m. deep purple shadows under the eyes of M. and B. told me how tired they were. At 3 a. m. neither girl could concentrate on the work. Their hands drifted over the beans and heavy eyelids drooped only to be jerked open every few minutes. Rose P., who worked beside me, said repeatedly, "I want to go to bed." Her eyes stared ahead at nothing in particular. Now and then a worker nudged her neighbor awake to keep her from slumping over the belt. Fatigue and the early morning chill made it almost impossible to concentrate on the work. Only a few women worked with attention. By four o'clock the fatigue was almost sickening. I stood up, I sat down, I ate some chocolate, drank water, anything to keep awake.

Work Beginning Before 6 a. m.

Though the law forbids work for women before 6 a. m., a third cannery habitually allowed women to begin hand-snipping of beans as early as 3 a. m. The necessity for increasing earnings because of the low rates, drove the women to work whenever they could, at whatever personal cost. Time cards for these women were always punched 7 a. m. although they had begun to work much earlier. Each day when the time clerk punched the investigator's card she told him that she had begun work before 6 a. m. His only answer was, "It's all right." This canner also permitted women, who began work at very early hours, to work until 7 or 8 o'clock at night, thus also violating the 10-hour law.

For the past three mornings, I have begun the hand-snipping of beans before 6 a. m. Yesterday I began work at 4 a. m. Today I was so sleepy at 3 a. m. I couldn't wake up. At 4 a. m. I forced myself to get out of bed and in the dark and cold of the early August morning, drank a cold glass of milk and hurried through the quiet streets of the town to the cannery. More than 40 Italian women and men were already at work at the large tables piled high with yellow beans. As on the previous morning, no one paid the slightest attention to my early arrival. I got an empty crate box and a chair and went quickly to work. I was so sleepy my head nodded frequently. I was so cold my hands were stiff and did the snipping of beans awkwardly. At 7 o'clock the American women came to work. Half of them sat at my table. "I came at 5 today," I told them. "Sure you can come at 3 or 2 o'clock if you want to, but I think too much of my sleep to come before 7," Mrs. P., a neatly dressed woman replied.

Hours of Piece-Workers Perfunctorily Recorded

The story of the investigator goes on to show that the factory hours of work were perfunctorily kept and gave no true picture of the piece workers' hours on the job.

At 7:15 a. m. the time clerk punched the time cards of each of the 115 women employed. "I began work at 5 today," I told him. Yesterday he had replied, "It's all right." Today he simply nodded his head and passed on to the next worker. When he had gone, I examined the cards of the women near me. "Mine is punched 7 a. m. too, but I came at five," I exclaimed to Mrs. B. and her sister sitting opposite me. "Oh, they punch 7 a. m. and 12 a. m., 12:45 and 5 p. m. It makes no difference because you can work from three in the morning to ten at night if there's work. I don't come before seven." At 3:30 this afternoon, after snipping beans from 5 a. m. to 2:45 p. m., Mr. A., the superintendent, told me I could work at the belt filling cans with beans. This I continued to do until 6:15 when the supply of snipped beans had been canned. I was at the factory for 13 hours today but only worked 12¼ hours; snipping beans by hand from 5 a. m. to 12 and from 12:15 to 2:45 p. m., when there was nothing for me to do for three quarters of an hour, and then filling cans from 3:30 to 6:15 p. m. The time cards, however, showed only 9¾ hours because they were punched 7 a. m. to 12; 12:45 to 2:45, and 3.30 to 6:15.

Unequal Distribution of Work Caused Illegal Hours

The necessity for increasing earnings owing to the low rates, led to rivalry for extra hours of work regardless of the ensuing physical strain. In two canneries an investigator saw women working more than 10 hours a day owing to careless distribution of work or favoritism. Sometimes during the afternoon, the superintendent selected for the extra hours women who had been employed longer and were better known to him, though others on hand whom he might have selected had worked a shorter time and would not have exceeded the legal limit.

About 4:30 yesterday, after working from 7 a. m., the women began asking if there would be evening work. About 5 o'clock Mr. B., the superintendent, singled out five women to whom he spoke briefly. When he had finished, the woman working beside me explained: "Those are old workers. He knows them a long time. He lets the ones he knows well stay at night." At 5:45 the rest of us were told there was no more work. I wanted to see how long the women would work after supper, so I remained with two girls who waited in the cannery for their father to come after them in his car. Shortly after 7 p. m. when the five women had returned to work on the belt, Mr. B. appeared. He noted the time for the women as he stood behind them. One of the girls said to me, "He don't always punch the time clock after seven. So he keeps the hours they work in that book." This morning I asked Helen B. what hour she quit work last night. "After eight," she said. "Do you punch a time clock after supper?" I asked. "Didn't last night," was her reply.

Concealment of Illegal Hours

In another cannery the hours were illegal as indicated by the following from the investigator's report.

At 12 midnight, the machine stopped. We went to the office and punched the time clock. My card read 12:06 a. m. Until the night watchman said he must lock the door, I warmed myself beside the large coal stove. On the wall beside the chimney were posted many yellow sheets of paper telling the daily hours of work for women. The top was dated today and read: 7:30 a. m. to 12; 1 to 6 p. m.; 6 to 9:30 p. m. "What are the yellow sheets for?" I asked the watchman. "Can't you read?" he asked me. "Sure, but I'm so sleepy I can't read straight." He looked at the sheets. "Oh, these are the daily reports of the hours the company works. It's for the Labor Inspector. He comes often in corn time." "But I worked until 12:06 a. m. this morning and it says 9:30 p. m." "Does it?" he asked. "Well, surely 9:30 looks better'n 12:06." He put out the light and locked the door.

In another instance on the other hand where the 10 hour day was violated, no effort was made to conceal the true record of hours. The time cards were punched accurately and one plaint paid time and a half for overtime beyond 10 hours.

Irregularity of Hours a Hardship

The irregularity of hours of work is another hardship to the women. There were instances when the good-will of the workers was stretched to the breaking point because the management failed to start work in the morning at a regular hour or at the hour indicated on the previous evening; or to indicate the number of hours they expected to work after 7 p. m. Three women became so provoked at this practice one day that they "simply didn't show up" the following morning. Incidentally, their absence held up, to the annoyance of the superintendent, the morning's anticipated output of canned beans.

"No one told us when to come today," Mrs. G., a housewife, said yesterday. "We women come at 7 a. m. because we began then yesterday, and the machines didn't begin today 'til 7:30 a. m. They tell us to come and when we get here they begin later. I'm going again to the superintendent and tell him I can't waste my time this way," Mrs. K. spoke emphatically.

The investigator herself reports:

I was the last woman to leave the cannery last night. When only the night watchman was left, I remembered I did not know what time to begin work on the morrow. I said to the watchman, "Oh, I forgot to ask what time to come tomorrow." "Well, the talk was to come back at 7 in the morning," he began, "maybe it was 7:30, but maybe you'd better come at 7 and make sure!"

Today I arrived at the cannery at 7:30 a. m. but the machines did not start running until 8. Mrs. K., Mrs. G., and one other woman did not come to work until afternoon.

When they were again working at the filling table, the superintendent came and scolded them for delaying the morning's output.

Better Management of Labor Supply Would Help in Solving this Problem

A description of the hours of work of women is not complete without reference to the canners' use of their labor supply. As we have seen they are still relying upon overtime employment and night work, sometimes illegally, to take care of an oversupply of raw material, and make a practice even of giving overtime work to favored employees, instead of bringing in a new shift of workers.

It is true that the plants are increasingly keeping lists of local help that can be called in. But from the observations of our investigation, there seemed to be no systematic effort to call in such workers for afternoon or evening work; on the contrary, the canners still find it easier to use their regular help.

This is probably due not only to a lack of management but also to the irregular hours and to the low wages paid in the industry, as will be shown in the next section of this report.

"They keep a list of people that want to work, but I ain't never seen 'em use 'em," one woman explained.

"There are plenty of women around here who'd work if they'd just be decently regular with their hours," was the rather unexpected answer of a man helper on one of the corn belts.

I worked until after midnight last night. Today I asked several women: "Why don't they have two shifts? Is it hard to get workers?" "Not hard, no; S., the superintendent would like two shifts, but I guess the owner's a stubborn fellow. 'You want work?' he says, 'Well here it is!' He don't care how long the hours are."

Wisconsin's Example

In contrast to the extreme irregularity of the hours and the great amount of overtime work in the New York canneries, the hours in the Wisconsin canneries, according to the reports of the Industrial Commission, are being held closely in line with the labor law. In that state the maximum hours for women are 60 per week, with not more than 11 hours on any one day. Wisconsin is also a large producer of peas, which are one of the most perishable of cannery products, and therefore has had to cope with the same problems as New York. The industry in Wisconsin is, however, making a more careful adjustment of acreage contracted for to fit the plant capacity and believes that still more can be done along this line. It has also put into effect a two-shift system of employment to help out in meeting emergencies. All of these schemes it is using in full co-operation with the State Industrial Commission.

LOW WAGE RATES

Since it was not possible, owing to the nature of the inquiry, to secure any information about wages from payrolls or management, our investigators made a special point while they were employed in the canneries of collecting all possible information on the hourly rates of their fellow workers. There was not much difficulty in doing this, since practically all the women in the rooms or sheds in which the investigators worked were paid at the same rate. We therefore have in hand the wage rates of over four hundred women.

FEMALES 16 YEARS OF AGE AND OVER

Rate Per Hour	Number of Workers
$.20	264
.22½	20
.25	116
.30	12

The predominating rate for sorting at the belt was 20 cents an hour. At 20 cents a woman working 51 hours a week, the legal limit permitted women in other lines of factory work, would earn $10.20. Everyone will admit that $10.20 is a meagre return for a 51-hour week, and there is little wonder that most workers welcome the extra hours up to 60 or 66 a week which make it possible for them to net $12 or $13.20. They will even work 14 hours a day to increase the daily wage by 40 cents. Yet it is not accurate to say they welcome the extra hours. They welcome the sorely needed extra pay and complain bitterly, as the reports of our investigators show, of their fatigue and exhaustion. No one digs more recklessly into her little capital, her health, than the low paid worker. Irregularity of work, which planning and good management can decrease, also encourages the women to take work whenever they can get it however long the hours.

How low the cannery wages are can be gauged to some extent

by comparison with those paid in another low-wage industry, namely, candy making. As the Consumers' League showed in its report, "Behind the Scenes in Candy Factories", the going wage in 1927 for beginners was $12.00 for a 48 to 54-hour week, although fairly often $14 was paid. Since the establishment of the candy White List in 1928, the beginning wage has been at least $14 in the 71 co-operating factories. This contrasts sharply with the $9.90 paid in canneries for the same length of hours, namely 49½.

While in the candy trade wages ordinarily increased with experience, and, in fact we found that 14% of the workers earned more than $20, there is no indication that a beginner's wage increases with experience during the cannery season, or from one season to another. To all intents and purposes, women are employed at the same processes year after year for the same rate without any difference for variation of skill. In only two instances in the canneries visited were women employed in any supervisory position at a higher wage.

The fact that certain canneries pay 25 cents an hour and even 30 cents an hour, at least for certain operations, proves that in this industry, as in every other industry, some employers believe higher wages pay.

In comparing the wages paid in New York canneries with those paid in California and Wisconsin, the most interesting facts are that New York in general pays a lower wage and does not pay an increased rate for overtime beyond the basic 48-hour week established by the hours law of 1927. The minimum time rate set by the Industrial Welfare Commission of California is 33⅓ cents an hour, and the minimum rate for overtime or work performed after the basic 8-hour day is rate and a quarter, or 41⅔ cents, and for all work performed after 12 hours double the basic rate, or 66⅔ cents an hour. Piece rates must yield to fifty per cent of the adult women working on them not less than the minimum time rates, and the canners themselves pay for the audit made by the State to see that this is done.

In Wisconsin the minimum rate set by the Industrial Commission is 25 cents an hour, except in places with a population of less than five thousand, where it is 22 cents. For overtime after the basic 9-hour day the minimum rate is 33 cents. This method of penalizing overtime work has been found to be effective in both these states in keeping down any very extensive use of long hours even in emergencies. In short, California and Wisconsin have discouraged long hours in the canneries rather than encouraged them as New York has done by its provisions for overtime and its lack of regulation of wages for such overtime.

Excerpts from the investigators' reports tell of the wages they found and the workers' reaction to them.

> Not until today, the second day at the sorting belt, did I learn that I was getting paid 20 cents an hour. The information came at 10:29 when the women were told, "No more work today." We had begun work at 8 a. m. having understood there were enough beans to keep us busy until night. Objections were many. Mrs. G., an old worker, was particularly annoyed. "Twenty cents an hour ain't enough. We should get 30 cents." Hannah P. was listening to her and said, "Trouble is, there isn't another factory in this place to make 'em raise wages!" Ruth D., of high school age and recently married, said, "If I had to work steady I'd ask for 30 cents. You can't live with 20 cents an hour. Last week I got $7.10 and Lucy, my chum, got six something."

> "They hold back one week's pay and pay on Wednesday. We get 20 cents an hour on beans and they say you get 25 cents on filling. It seems kinda little. The work ain't hard, but it's awful tiresome. I think they ought to pay 30 cents an hour. I've worked here four weeks and I haven't drawed a full week's pay yet. Week before last I drew $6.30. We ain't worked regular since I've been here."

> "But I haven't drawn $12 a week since I've been here on peas; $10.50 is the most I've got. Last week my pay

was $2.50. We worked only two nights until 6 o'clock. Not enough to pay for the baby's milk. Twenty cents an hour isn't enough."

"When we work less'n 10 hours (a day) I get less'n $2. Two dollars ain't enough for 10 hours. Workin' at the belt gets you so tired. Some factories pay more for overtime. We ought to get more'n 25 cents regular, and more for overtime."

That the women have tried to get higher wages is shown in the following sketches.

"Last year the women tried to strike for more pay. Half stayed in, so we couldn't do nothing."

B. told us today of the strike of the Italian women two years ago for 22½ cents an hour. "They were getting 20 cents an hour. It was right while the tomatoes were waiting for them in the ketchup house. The boss told them to go back to Buffalo for he wouldn't pay more. But he didn't think they'd go. They packed up and asked for the trucks to take them. So he paid them 22½ cents an hour, but this year it's only 20 cents.

Some of the American women said that the low piece rate and low hourly rate were based on the willingness of the Italian women to do the wet, unpleasant, and monotonous work of peeling tomatoes, cutting beets, and snipping beans for long hours.

The company pays 1½ cents a pound for hand snipping of beans. A comparison of the hourly earnings made by Italian and American women shows that the Italian makes more. At 10 a. m. No. . . ., a very fast Italian woman, said she had made $1.86. She said she began work at 3:30 a. m. If she did she made .286 cents an hour. Her friend said, "She works like a dog. She fills many boxes of beans, yes;

but she is thin and maybe get sick by 'n by." The most that Nora H. made an hour was 16 cents. An Italian woman working beside me made 21 cents an hour for the first three hours of work. One old Italian woman made 26 cents an hour snipping beans by hand. When she mentioned the amount she added, "But I've worked steady ten hours and now I'm good for nothing but bed." "Them Italians set the wages. They work hard for any pay. If American women want work they got to take the same here."

By 2 p. m. the piles of beans on the eight tables were nearly leveled. The women began calling, "Tony, more beans. We want more beans to snip." After Tony had dumped two boxes on our nearly empty table, we asked for more. "All, all," he yelled. "No more beans today, all you get." The women at our table persisted. The woman to my left yelled to him in Italian. Tony's face darkened and he replied angrily. The woman hurled her answer. Tony came to the edge of the table, shouting and waving his arms. When he was gone, the new girl asked, "What does he say?" "He says he don't give the Italian women from Buffalo more beans than us. But I tell him he does. He always does. He not fair. His wife at one table. He's a beast. I hate him." It is the daily answer of many women. Tony's "game of favoritism" as it is called among the women. One has but to compare the big pile of beans on the two center tables with the low piles on the other six at any time of the day to know why the women "hate" him.

When Tony dumps a box of beans on one of the six tables, he also dumps one on each of the two center tables. I have watched him each day. He edges near the crates of beans piled on the hand truck. When every woman has a few beans to keep her busy, he quickly dumps the extra crates on the two center "Buffalo" tables, still covered with enough beans to keep the women snipping until five o'clock. Mrs. P.

was infuriated at Tony's action. "If it wasn't for them Italians we'd get decent wages. They take anything you give them. They'll work for a cent and a half a pound. That's why we American women have to."

As the tomatoes fell from the blanching machine into pans, Joe, the foreman, knew which pan contained a greater amount of good tomatoes. The Italian women got the best always. The helper brought me and other American women, pans of cold, green, blemished tomatoes, until we protested. Some of the Italian women were so skillful and got such clean tomatoes that all of their pails were whole tomatoes.

In plants where the American workers on the machines spoke against the low wage, the management threatened to replace them with Italians who would accept less.

The foreman talked today about wages to two of the younger women operating husking machines. He was telling about the owner, who had passed through the husking room a few minutes before. "He's a high-hatter," he said, "owns five canneries. He only paid 20 cents to the women before we got the machines. They're new this year. When he decided to put American girls on them I said, "Pay 'em 30 cents an hour and I'll see they work." "But why 30 cents an hour?" asked one of the women, "why not 35 or 40?" But he don't have to pay 30 cents. Why those Italians will come for 20 cents any day we say."

Why don't they pay the girls as much as men?" one woman asked the foreman. "Cause they don't have to. If the American women don't take what we give, we can get all the Italians we want at 20 cents an hour."

HOUSING FOR IMPORTED WORKERS

For many years the canners having plants near small towns have made a practice of bringing workers, largely Italians and Poles, from the large industrial centers to increase their labor supply. Whole families come for this summer migration and live in the quarters furnished by the canners. According to the reports of previous investigations, the accommodations were in most cases found to be wretched and without proper sanitary provisions. Although it was not possible for our investigators to make a thorough study of the housing problem last summer, some account of their observations will be given.

A half mile down the dusty road we come to two one-story tenements, "row-houses," of the cheapest construction, unpainted and dilapidated. They are about 25 feet apart and although Mrs. S. tells me "one row of houses has been put in order by the company" one tenement looks as unfit for habitation as the other. Between the two houses a water pipe sticks two feet out of the ground. Piled about it are broken crate boxes and tree limbs to be used as firewood. "That's where we get our water," the Polish woman tells me. "Water and wood is free." The interior of the three small rooms where Mrs. S. and her four children live, has been "put in order." The peeling white-wash exposes the dust and stain of former seasons and signs of dampness appear on the wall and cracks under the windows. The cookstove is too heavy for the floor and the corner where it stands sags down, causing the chimney to lean and give off smoke while dinner is being cooked. "It's not so bad as the empty homes," explains Marie the 14-year-old daughter. "But it's so hard to keep clean. I scrub and clean while mama is at the factory."

"The doors and windows don't fit," Mr. S. says, "they let in flies when it's hot and wind when it's cold. Can't keep warm." "Where do the flies come from?" I ask. "From the garbage over there on the road," is the answer. "Company doesn't take it away once a week but says it will."

Marie shows me the two straw mattresses, one in each of the two tiny rooms directly behind the kitchen. They fill the rooms, are wedged in between the wooden walls, one on a sagging wooden frame, the other on a broken-down iron bedstead. There are two small windows. "Five of you live here?" I ask. "Six until last week," Mr. S. replies. "My boy, he sleep on the floor 'til the mice won't let him sleep."

During the noon hour I watched Italian children playing in the yard about the cannery camp situated on a hill opposite the factory.

"What are the houses like?" I ask the engineer. "They're cut up into apartments of various sizes for the Italian families. If I had a dog I cared anything about I wouldn't let him live in those shacks. The mattresses are mouldy. They've been there for years."

Two days later I go to the camp to see for myself how the Buffalo people live, and to talk to the Italian woman "boss" of the colony. In the middle of the yard is a pile of decaying garbage. The stench is sickening and hundreds of flies swarm upon it. Near by, three small children are playing. I find the "boss" of the camp standing over a boiling hot cook stove. Reluctantly she answers my questions and permits me to see a few of the three-room apartments. "No garbage cans," she explains. "City takes away when wants to. Sometimes once a week, sometimes two weeks. Not my business to watch garbage, I watch children while mama work in cannery. I see nobody comes in houses while all work in day time."

"Workers all come from Buffalo. Company pay railroad back if stay all season. Seventeen families live in house.

Yes, rooms too small for family. When fire in kitchen nobody stays in house, stove so hot. Everybody stay outdoors 'til go to bed." "Wood and water free? Yes. Baths? Men wash in cannery; women get water from faucet in pans. Don't wash many times. Go sometime to lake over far hill—Sundays maybe." The three-room apartments she shows me are all alike. The kitchen and two sleeping rooms are so small that only one person at a time can pass around the cook stove; and one must crawl over a bed in order to get into it. There is no space for a table in the kitchen and pans containing berry pulp have been put on the beds and braced against the window sills to get them out of the way. There they attract hundreds of flies. Heavy wire grating is nailed over the window spaces in which there are no glass panes. There is so little light in the kitchen that the condition of the walls and ceilings cannot be seen."

The deplorable conditions revealed here agree in practically all details with those found years ago in the cannery camps. It is clear that no lasting changes were made and that today the quarters, so far as we observed them, are just as neglected as they were at the time of the Factory Investigating Commission's study.

Yet a practical method for providing facilities that are decent and offer at least a minimum of comfort has been worked out. A cannery housing code is included under the Rules of the Industrial Board. Also, more recently, the State Conservation Commission in managing the tourist camps in the state parks has set up a standard which the canners might well study. For every family in the camp it supplies at least one connection with a water supply of tested quality, a fireplace with wood supply, and covered garbage can, contents of which are removed at least once a day. There are also within easy reach, well-constructed comfort stations which are kept clean and sanitary. These are the elementary provisions for decent living which the state provides for the hundreds of persons seeking summer recreation in the parks.

Is it too much to ask that the canners should provide at least these minima for the workers whom they bring from their homes and lodge on their own premises?

WHAT SHOULD BE DONE?

In view of all the facts set forth in this account of New York canneries, it is clear that much thought must be given to improving the conditions of work and all that affects personnel, and adequate remedial measures taken, if this industry is to measure up to any fair standard of factory management. The hourly rate of wages is too low. Third, some effective means must be found to regularize hours of work and keep overtime within reasonable bounds. Recognizing that even the most efficient management sometimes contends with unforeseen difficulties which contribute to long hours, the Consumers' League still believes that there are several ways here as in other states in which these difficulties may be met. This problem it seems to us may be attacked from various angles.

How Hours of Work Can be Regularized

Better Use of Labor Supply. To the extent that long hours are due to lack of proper recruiting and lack of proper use of the labor supply to meet the needs of the cannery, the Consumers' League suggests the following.

That before the season begins each plant should make up a list of names and addresses of all available workers in the locality far more exhaustively than has been the practice up to the present time, and make use of this list for employing the regular force as well as for working up a list of persons on reserve to be called in for emergencies.

A special agent, other than the superintendent, should be in charge of this work, whose name should be sent to the Industrial Commissioner before the season begins, as it should be through this agent that the company should co-operate with the Commissioner in seeing that all the provisions of the labor law are obeyed.

The appointment of such an agent is an innovation in New York State, but it is the very effective measure required by the Industrial Board of Wisconsin to control especially the hours of cannery work. With a better use of the labor supply under the supervision mentioned here, it should be possible at rush times to obtain two shifts of workers, which are now regularly installed in the Wisconsin canneries handling perishable materials, and thus avoid the present practice of keeping at work in the evening people who have already worked the legal hours.

Also, if through this procedure, hours of work were regular and if notice were always given in advance of the exact hours for beginning work—when there is necessary variation in the schedule—there would without doubt be a more stable labor force, attending with greater regularity, and feeling a greater responsibility toward their jobs.

Possibility of Controlling the Supply of Raw Materials. While there is no doubt that putting into operation an efficient two-shift system is the most immediate method for cutting down the overtime in New York canneries, yet the situation calls for intensive study along other lines. Nothing that has been done in this state seems as yet to have struck at the root of the matter, although the experimentation that is going on in other states indicates very clearly that more can be done if proper attention is given.

In so far as the cause of overtime work is due to an attempt to handle a varying supply of raw material, with the result that during rush periods the capacity of the plant is exceeded and overtime and night work frequently employed, we suggest that there are possible ways in which the supplies may be more effectively controlled. More effort should be made to have the planting and harvesting and especially the delivery of crops regulated so that oversupplies will not be delivered to the cannery. In spite of difficulties due to varying weather conditions, farmers and canneries can work in closer co-operation to bring a more even flow of produce to the plant. Under the same conditions, Wisconsin has found through actual experience that acreage for which they contract can be made to more closely approximate the capacity of the plant and supplies can be better regulated. Even holding them one night allows more leeway in getting them through the sorting process for which the women are employed.

In recent years, as we all know, it has been found possible to bring peas from Florida and California in remarkably fresh condition to the New York market. Does this not indicate at least that the possibilities of cold storage at the cannery as a resource in emergencies has not been fully tried out?

Higher Wages for Overtime. Management would presumably make greater efforts to eliminate overtime if it had to pay higher rates for it as in California and Wisconsin.

Fair Wage Rates Should Be Agreed On

We found wages in most cases are at the very low level of 20 cents an hour; no higher rate is paid for overtime, and no increase is given for greater experience or skill.

No able industrialists hold briefs for depressed wages. It is poor management to have wages which the imported labor is willing to accept made the basis for the wage scale.

If the Canners' Association would determine in co-operation with the Industrial Commissioner what are fair wages for the various operations and fair overtime rates beyond the basic 48 hour week, probably the majority of the industry would pay these wages.

In another low-wage industry—candy making—at the suggestion of the Consumers' League a minimum wage of not less than $14 to beginners for a full week is now being voluntarily paid by at least 71 manufacturers. These wages represent a considerable advance for many manufacturers.

Better Working Conditions Would Increase Production

Equipment. So far as machinery is concerned, much has been found that is antiquated, in poor repair, or ill adjusted for the job. Especially the jolting and shaking of conveyors, as noted in the report, wears out the workers and makes their jobs far more fatiguing than need be. It hardly seems necessary to point out that a thorough checking up and the making of repairs or remodelling of all such equipment are of prime importance.

Seating. In checking up the technical equipment of the factory, the problem of seating the workers should be newly considered, with full knowledge of the relation between seats and the machine and the type of work to be performed. In cannery work, as in all other factory employment, bad seating adds appreciably to the tiredness of the workers. It decreases their efficiency and visibly affects the quality of the product. When thought is given to this problem, as has been done by forward-looking management, it has been found possible in other industries to have women comfortably seated at their jobs. In the best arrangements, as required by California cannery law, chairs are adjusted to the work tables or the machines in such a way that the worker can either sit or stand, and in both cases her relation to the work is substantially the same. To make this possible in New York canneries there is need of much new seating equipment in almost all the plants visited, and also of considerable rebuilding in removing obstructions under tables and at machines which now interfere with the proper posture of the workers.

Rest Periods. Experience in other industries shows that especially for repetitive processes, among which may be included cannery work, rest periods of 10 to 15 minutes, in the middle of the work time, both morning and afternoon, refresh the worker and undoubtedly stimulate production.

Noise. In view of our new knowledge of the effect of noise on health and efficiency, especially in industry, the inattention to noise of machines and the shock from use of live steam for cleaning which we found in the canneries shows that changes are much needed. In well-regulated plants the sorting tables for women are placed at some distance from machines, and often separated from them by partitions as well. If employers realized how much they handicapped their workers through subjecting them to constant noise, they would without doubt make every effort to eliminate it.

Exposure. Similarly our stories show the advisability of scrutinizing very carefully all parts of the working environment and devising methods of giving far better protection to the workers. Good practice would certainly consist in seeing that they were not subjected to cold, to rapid changes in temperature, and to draughts, in the factories, nor to wind and storm in the sheds. There are remedies both simple and practical for these conditions.

In addition, it is not too much to expect that the floors where the women work should be free from water, or that effective slats and foot rests should be provided that will keep their feet dry. Likewise, in order to remove the possibility of having the water leak down upon the women from tables and machines, as is often the case now, equipment should be overhauled, or replaced. In processes where there is unavoidable moisture or spraying of juices over the workers, it is but fair that management should provide waterproof aprons or other protection.

Cannery Camps. Gross defects in housing should be remedied. There is need of new construction, better sanitation, and a thorough clean-up of the quarters provided for immigrant workers. Only constant policing of such premises will bring about lasting improvement.

Titles in This Series

10 *Risks for the Single Woman in the City, An Anthology of Studies by Late Nineteenth-Century Reformers*. David J. and Sheila M. Rothman, eds. New York, 1986

11 *Saving Babies: Children's Bureau Studies of Infant Mortality, 1913–1917*. David J. and Sheila M. Rothman, eds. New York, 1986

12 *The Sheppard-Towner Act, the Record of the Hearings*. David J. and Sheila M. Rothman, eds. New York, 1986

13 *Women in Prison, 1834–1928, An Anthology of Pamphlets from the Progressive Movement*. David J. and Sheila M. Rothman, eds. New York, 1986

14 Azel Ames, Jr., *Sex in Industry: A Plea for the Working Girl*, Boston, 1875

15 Robert South Barrett, *The Care of the Unmarried Mother*, Alexandria, 1929

16 Elizabeth Blackwell, M.D., *The Laws of Life, with Special Reference to the Physical Education of Girls*, New York, 1852

17 Alida C. Bower and Ruth S. Bloodgood, *Institutional Treatment of Delinquent Boys*, Washington, D.C., 1935–36

18 New York Assembly, *The Girls of the Department Store*, New York, 1895

19 Committee on the Infant and Preschool Child, *Nursery Education*, New York, 1931

20 Robert Latou Dickinson and Lura Beam, *The Single Woman: A Medical Study in Sex Education*, Baltimore, 1934

21 G. V. Hamilton, M.D., *A Research in Marriage*, New York, 1929

22 Elizabeth Harrison, *A Study of Child Nature from the Kindergarten Standpoint*, Chicago, 1909

23 Orie Latham Hatcher, *Rural Girls in the City for Work*, Richmond, 1930

24 William Healy, Augusta F. Bronner, et al., *Reconstructing Behavior in Youth*, New York, 1929

25 Henry H. Hibbs, Jr., *Infant Mortality: Its Relation to Social and Industrial Conditions*, New York, 1916

26 *The Juvenile Court Record*, Chicago, 1900, 1901

27 Mary A. Livermore, *What Shall We Do With Our Daughters?* Boston, 1883

28 *Massachusetts Society for the Prevention of Cruelty to Children: First Ten Annual Reports*, Boston, 1882

29 Maude E. Miner, *Slavery of Prostitution: A Plea for Emancipation*, New York, 1916

30 Maud Nathan, *The Story of an Epoch-Making Movement*, New York, 1926

31 National Florence Crittenton Mission, *Fourteen Years' Work Among "Erring Girls,"* Washington, D.C., 1897

32 New York Milk Committee, *Reducing Infant Mortality in the Ten Largest Cities in the United States*, New York, 1912

33 James Orton, ed., *The Liberal Education of Women: The Demand and the Method*, New York, 1873

34 Margaret Reeves, *Training Schools for Delinquent Girls*, New York, 1929

35 Ben L. Reitman, M.D., *The Second Oldest Profession*, New York, 1931

36 John Dale Russell and Associates, *Vocational Education*, Washington, D.C., 1938

37 William H. Slingerland, *Child Welfare Work in California*, New York, 1916

38 William H. Slingerland, *Child Welfare Work in Pennsylvania*, New York, 1917

39 *Documents Relative to the House of Refuge, Instituted by the Society for the Reformation of Juvenile Delinquents in the City of New York, in 1824*, New York, 1832

40 George S. Stevenson, M.D., and Geddes Smith, *Child Guidance Clinics*, New York, 1934

41 Henry Winfred Thurston, *Delinquency and Spare Time*, New York, 1918

42 U.S. National Commission on Law Observance and Enforcement, *Report on Penal Institutions, Probation and Parole*, Washington, D.C., 1931

43 Miriam Van Waters, *Parents on Probation*, 1927

44 Ira S. Wile, M.D., *The Sex Life of the Unmarried Adult*, New York, 1934

45 Helen Leland Witmer, *Psychiatric Clinics for Children*, New York, 1940

46 Young Women's Christian Association, *First Ten Annual Reports, 1871–1880*, New York, 1871–1880